THE

ENCORE

MARK SANBORN is an internationally acclaimed keynote speaker and bestselling author. LeadershipGurus.net lists him as one of the top leadership gurus in the world today. His numerous books include the bestsellers *The Fred Factor: How Passion in Your Work and Life Can Turn the Ordinary into the Extraordinary* and *You Don't Need a Title to Be a Leader: How Anyone Anywhere Can Make a Positive Difference.*

Mark has presented over 2,000 speeches in the U.S. and abroad. He holds the Certified Speaking Professional (CSP) designation from the National Speakers Association and is a member of the Speaker Hall of Fame (CPAE). He is a past president of the National Speakers Association and winner of the Cavett, the highest award given by that organization. He has been awarded the Ambassador of Free Enterprise Award by Sales & Marketing Executives International.

His live presentations include:

- The Encore Effect: How to Give a Remarkable Performance
- The Fred Factor: How to Make the Ordinary Extraordinary
- You Don't Need a Title to Be a Leader

For more information, visit www.marksanborn.com
or call 001-800-650-3343.

For free resources to complement this book, go to
www.theencoreeffect.com.

THE
ENCORE EFFECT

How to Achieve
Remarkable Performance
in Anything You Do

MARK SANBORN

BUSINESS
BOOKS

Published by Random House Business Books 2009

2 4 6 8 10 9 7 5 3 1

Copyright © Mark Sanborn 2009

First published in the United States in 2008 by Doubleday

First published in Great Britain in 2009 by
Random House Business Books
Random House, 20 Vauxhall Bridge Road,
London SW1V 2SA

www.rbooks.co.uk

Addresses for companies within The Random House Group Limited can be found at:
www.randomhouse.co.uk/offices.htm

The Random House Group Limited Reg. No. 954009

A CIP catalogue record for this book
is available from the British Library

ISBN 9781847940353

The Random House Group Limited supports The Forest Stewardship Council (FSC),
the leading international forest certification organisation. All our titles that are
printed on Greenpeace approved FSC certified paper carry the FSC logo. Our paper
procurement policy can be found at www.rbooks.co.uk/environment

Mixed Sources

Product group from well-managed
forests and other controlled sources
www.fsc.org   Cert no. TT-COC-2139
© 1996 Forest Stewardship Council

Design by Diane Hobbing of Snap-Haus Graphics

Printed in Great Britain by CPI Bookmarque, Croydon, CR0 4TD

To my remarkable friend and mentor
Charlie "Tremendous" Jones

CONTENTS

PART THREE
Sharing the Encore Effect

ACKNOWLEDGMENTS

Thanks to . . .

. . . my editor Roger Scholl for his able and friendly assistance and to my publisher Michael Palgon, as well as the team at Doubleday. I appreciate our partnership.

. . . my literary agent and friend Sealy Yates.

. . . William Kruidenier for his editorial assistance.

. . . my friends Mark Shupe, Rauna May, Julie Marks Miller, and Robert Tucker for their input and encouragement.

. . . the team at Sanborn & Associates, Inc., especially Maritza Tamburelli and Tom Gray.

. . . my family: Dorothy Sanborn, Shawn and Shana Sanborn, and Bill and Shelly Wadkins.

My love and appreciation as always goes to my beautiful bride Darla and my sons Hunter and Jackson, the great joys of my life.

Soli Deo Gloria

THE
ENCORE EFFECT

WARNING!

When reading *The Encore Effect* . . .

1. You may find yourself thinking, "I already knew that."

   That's good!

   That means you're a step ahead in the game, ready to move toward what is most important in life: applying what you know. It's not what we know in life that matters most, but what we do with what we know.

2. You may find yourself disagreeing with something I've written.

   Wonderful!

   That shows you're reading thoughtfully and evaluating what you've read as you go. I don't want to convert you to my way of thinking. My hope is to challenge your beliefs and stimulate your thinking. When honest people disagree, change is usually the result—often change for the better.

3. You may conclude that something I suggest would never work for you.

   Not a problem!

   A large part of finding what works best begins with eliminating what doesn't work.

   You and I are different people—we undoubtedly have different personalities, temperaments, strengths, weaknesses, and comfort levels. My goal is to encourage you to achieve results, not dictate to you how to achieve them. But I would ask you to remember that the ideas in this book have proven beneficial for a lot of people. So I urge you to give them a fair hearing.

4. You may think, "I could score points with my boss (or spouse or colleague) with this or that idea."

That is not the best way to use this book.

People who are successful and effective in the long run act out of their own core convictions, not those of others. The worst way to use this book is merely to pull out one or two ideas that you think will enhance the perceptions others have of you.

By skimming this book quickly looking for pearls, you may shortchange the thirty-day process that psychologists say is necessary to effect real change in our lives. I would rather you read slowly and "chew on" the ideas. Take notes in the back of the book or in a journal.

5. The journey is the destination.

This book is not an end-all. It is not Mark Sanborn's quick fix for your life and career. Reading it is a process of discovery and application. I'm a fellow traveler on the road to effectiveness, and I've written *The Encore Effect* to share the lessons I've learned so far (and I look forward to hearing about yours at www.marksanborn.com). I hope that what you encounter in these pages will make at least a small contribution to your own journey to remarkable performance.

INTRODUCTION

What if . . . ?

What if you were so good at your work, such an asset to your company, that your employer would do almost anything not to lose you?

What if you performed in such a way that people buzzed about your performance and wanted more of your time, ideas, participation, and leadership?

When people constantly demand more and more of whatever it is you do, this is what I describe as the Encore Effect.

You know what an encore is. In fact, you've probably been responsible for a couple. You go to a concert and are so moved by the performance that you and the rest of the audience start clapping, cheering, and yelling, "Bravo!"—refusing to let the artist or performer leave the stage. The audience, prepared to applaud all night if necessary, implores the artist to perform one more number.

And when the artist relents and performs one more piece, the call for an encore begins all over again. A second encore and then a third are called for, and many times the weary, but appreciative, artist complies.

What if that artist was you? I don't mean that you are necessarily a singer or musician or actor—not all of us are gifted in those ways. But each of us performs on a stage of one sort or another—an office, a sales floor, an assembly line, a pulpit, a classroom, a playing field, a home, a showroom, a hospital. Whatever

stage you perform on, it can be just as worthy of an encore performance as any concert hall in the world.

I believe that a worthy goal in life is to have people shouting
for more of whatever it is we do that is really important and
matters to us. The world is desperately looking for people who
make such a difference, who produce memorable results, who
have a positive impact on others. Such "performers" make
themselves indispensable. Whatever their stage, they shine.

That is the power, and the promise, of the Encore Effect.

PART ONE

Understanding
the
Encore Effect

CHAPTER 1

THE POWER OF
ENCORE PERFORMANCES

All the world's a stage,
And all the men and women merely players.
They have their exits and their entrances,
And one man in his time plays many parts,
His acts being seven ages.

—WILLIAM SHAKESPEARE, *AS YOU LIKE IT*, ACT II, SCENE 7

In Shakespeare's comedy *As You Like It*, Jaques seems to think we move through life controlled by a preordained script, with little or no control, making our "exits" and "entrances" by divine cue. I couldn't disagree with him more. While I wholly subscribe to the idea of the divine in our lives, I recognize that my life is a performance that I'm in charge of.

We all have roles to play. Our performance at work, and in every other aspect of our life, is a public display of our very best self. And if we're true to ourselves, we never have to remember what part we played with whom. We don't have to check our notes to see what the people are expecting from our callback performance.

To make your performance better, according to the legendary founder of Southwest Airlines, Herb Kelleher, you "change your practices, not your *principles*." In other words, you don't have to change who you are. Different people can be successful in very different ways.

"My best lesson in leadership came during my early days as a trial lawyer," says Kelleher. "Wanting to learn from the best, I went to see two of the most renowned litigators in San Antonio try cases. One sat there and never objected to anything, was very gentle with witnesses, and established a rapport with the jury. The other was an aggressive, thundering hell-raiser. And both seemed to win every case. That's when I realized there are many different paths, not one right path. That's true of leadership as well. People with different personalities, different approaches, or different values succeed not because one set of values or practices is superior, but because their values and practices are genuine. And when you and your organization are true to yourselves—when you deliver results and a singular experience—customers can spot it from thirty thousand feet."

We all perform various roles in our lives on the stage of life. But those roles should be different expressions of our best self.

Our performances matter. They can have a powerful impact on those around us. As parents, our performance shapes and influences our children. As employees and managers, our performance can make our company better, move a project forward, spark ideas among colleagues, and influence customers.

When I was sixteen, I learned that Og Mandino was scheduled to speak in Akron, Ohio, about a ninety-minute drive from my home. Og is one of the best-selling self-help authors of all time, and I had already devoured several of his books, including *The Greatest Salesman in the World* and *The Greatest Miracle in the*

World. Rookie driver or not, I was determined to go hear him speak.

In the course of the speech, Og talked about his troubled past; at one point he seriously considered ending his life. He spoke about the influences that had lifted him out of despair and set him on the road to remarkable achievement.

His delivery was low-key, but his message was powerful and sincere, and it inspired me. I came away determined to work harder and better in my own life. Others seemed to feel the same way—at the end of his talk the audience gave Og a standing ovation. I was witnessing the Encore Effect in action.

The ideas and passion with which Og Mandino spoke planted the seeds of change in me. The performance made me *act*.

And that is the potential impact of a remarkable performance. It can change the lives of those around you. That is the kind of experience we all want to have. And that's why creating a remarkable performance is so key to personal success.

Since that day spent listening to Og Mandino, I have observed performances of every kind throughout the United States and abroad. From Broadway to corporate boardrooms, I've learned that every remarkable performance affects us. They:

Move us to act.
Make us feel good.
Cause us to laugh.
Stimulate us to think.

Only the most incredible performances accomplish all four, but over time I've learned that every remarkable performance achieves at least one of these four impacts.

I've seen plenty of performances that have disappointed me,

and I'm sure you have too—in corporate offices, restaurants, department stores, and churches, at car rental agencies, at ticket counters and security lines at airports, and in every other conceivable venue or location.

And, yes, I've been guilty of disappointing performance. In college I ran for a major office in an organization to which I belonged. I was defeated. In the aftermath I was asked to chair an important committee. I had no passion for the work of the committee, but I didn't want to look like a sore loser so I accepted the role. I am ashamed to say that I did a terrible job. I did, however, learn an important lesson: it is difficult if not impossible to be remarkable at doing something you don't have your heart in.

But coming face-to-face with my own disappointing performances has spurred me on to act differently and better the next time.

A remarkable performance, on the other hand, moves us and makes us want more.

My vocation as a professional speaker puts me on stages several times every week. The issue of performance is a front-burner reality for me.

But in fact, all of us, like Broadway performers, are called to be "on" all the time—to give our best performance as individuals, spouses, parents, employees, or bosses. Whatever stage we find ourselves on, most of us are called to perform every day. We need to be remarkable, regardless of how we feel.

If I asked three people in your life—for example, your boss, a customer, and a family member—to use one word to describe your performance in life, what word would they choose?

Would they describe you as . . .

Disappointing?
Marginal?
Fair?
Okay?
Good?
Excellent?
Great?

These responses run the gamut, from the negative to the positive. But there is one response that I don't hear very often: "His (her) performance is so amazing that I would do whatever it took to keep him (or her) on my team."

What kinds of words might describe such a performance?

Amazing
Remarkable
Unbelievable
Unique
One of a kind
Inimitable
Awesome
Extraordinary
Phenomenal
Incredible

Those are the kinds of words we might use to describe the performance of an artist who is called back for an encore. And they are the kinds of words we should want others to use to describe our own performance in life.

There is one word that embodies all of these adjectives, with no need for an exclamation point: *remarkable*.

I believe all of us would like to have our performance described as remarkable. All of us would like to excel at the things that matter most to us. And it is by giving such performances that we achieve the Encore Effect.

Larger Than Life

My friend Charlie "Tremendous" Jones is larger than life. He is loud and loving, boisterous and caring, someone who "lives large." When people first meet Charlie, many of them probably wonder, "Is this guy for real?" Trust me—Charlie is for real. He is totally authentic.

Charlie is a big man in size and in spirit. He loves people. As his nickname of many years suggests, he believes that *life is tremendous*.

I mention Charlie because larger-than-life people often have something important to teach us. They demonstrate that there can be more to life than we typically experience. Their personalities and behaviors jar us out of ordinary thinking and show us that, if we choose, we can be bigger, better, and bolder than we've been. They can snap us out of our plain-vanilla existence and invite us to live on a higher plane.

How can each of us make our own performance bigger, better, and bolder? How can we make it remarkable?

Read on, because that is exactly what this book is about.

CHAPTER 2

FROM ROUTINE
TO REMARKABLE—
MAKE THEM WANT MORE!

A long line forms early on Saturday mornings every week from April to November in Matthews, North Carolina—rain or shine, hot or cold.

The crowd is not lining up for concert tickets, a department store sale, or the latest digital device. They're lining up for Sammy Koenigsberg's fresh-picked, organically grown vegetables.

Matthews is a small, historic community that has been engulfed by the city of Charlotte's metropolitan sprawl. Part of its charm is the farmers' market that runs from late April to November in a small, empty lot in the heart of the town. No buying or selling is allowed until the bell rings at 7:15 A.M.

Get to the Matthews market before 7:00, however, and you'll see a line of twenty to thirty people in front of Sammy's waiting to hand over their money. Almost as soon as Sammy gets his produce unloaded and onto his tables, folks fill their bags and get in line to wait for the 7:15 bell.

Why do people get out of their warm, comfortable beds at daybreak on Saturday morning to stand in line to give Sammy their money? Because he gives them an encore performance every week with fresh produce that is out of this world.

Understand: it isn't just about the quality of Sammy's *produce*; it's about the quality of Sammy's *performance*. Yes, the produce is less than twenty-four hours old, from growing in the field to available at the stand. Compare that against the seven- to twelve-day-old produce you'll find at most grocery stores.

His customers count on Sammy to be there every Saturday. They know not only what they'll find, but who will be there. It helps to know the producer. Such knowledge of how Sammy grows his organic food is reassuring, and he's available for any questions customers might have.

Often, Sammy's wife and some of his eight children help out. By getting to know Sammy's family, many customers feel like they become part of the extended family. And Sammy's regular customers are invited to visit his farm, where he takes great pride in the beauty of his gardens.

It would be silly to say that any produce has "personality." In a blind comparison test, I doubt if even regulars would know the difference between Sammy's and store-bought vegetables. But people buy from people, and what's remarkable is that Sammy's personality and way of doing business *become* the difference—

the kind of eyes-wide-open difference that makes people consistently come back for more of what he provides.

Says one customer I know, "Sammy has a winsome, gentle personality; he's more than happy to talk to customers about his produce—or anything else. Never in a hurry, always takes time for the people who pay his bills."

You might ask, how much does Sammy spend on marketing and advertising? When you have people lining up for the privilege of buying your products, how much advertising do you have to do? Sammy sells everything he produces on the basis of satisfied customer referrals and repeat business. He's a living example of the Encore Effect: deliver a remarkable product in a remarkable way and you'll have people coming back for more.

Think about Sammy and his enthusiastic customers the next time you sit through a mind-numbing stream of product commercials on TV. Sure, advertising has its place. It helps us learn about new products and their features and benefits. But how many products out there are "encore" products—products you would line up at 6:45 A.M. to buy before the store runs out of them? Not many.

You may never meet Sammy Koenigsberg, but you can't have missed an example of the Encore Effect at the national level last year. On June 29, 2007, Apple, Inc., and AT&T retail stores opened their doors to let in the long lines of customers who had been waiting for hours to hand over up to $599 for an iPhone. Yes, many of these early customers were the Apple faithful who will buy anything with the bite-missing Apple logo on it. But the Microsoft faithful did the same thing on September 25, 2007, the release date for *Halo 3*; this latest version of the shoot-'em-up game that plays on the Xbox 360 machine racked up

$170 million in sales the first day, and $300 million the first week. Games like *Halo* might not be your personal choice—they aren't mine—but there is always a hungry audience for an encore product or performance.

Why do people line up for the privilege of giving their hard-earned money to others? Because they're getting something remarkable in return! What they are getting has more perceived value to them than the money itself. And in life, value is in the eye of the beholder.

Routine or Remarkable?

In the previous chapter, the key word was "performance." A performance, according to the *American Heritage Dictionary*, is the way someone or something functions. A common way to think of a performance is in terms of what someone does on a stage for purposes of entertainment. But that's a subcategory. At the core, a performance is simply the way someone or something performs—they way they do what they do.

What kinds of performances produce the "once is enough" effect versus the Encore Effect?

Forget the Bell

Anyone who's been through high school algebra knows what a bell-shaped curve looks like and what it represents. If you were absent that day, you at least remember the expression "grading on the curve." Teachers graded "on the curve" when everybody's performance on a test was so bad that the grades had to be spread out in a normal distribution:

Top 5 percent of students get an A
Next highest 10 percent get a B
Next highest 70 percent get a C
Next highest 10 percent get a D
Lowest 5 percent get an F

The assumption on a bell-curve distribution is that the greatest number of people in any setting—a class, a university, a nation—are "average" people. They are hardworking, upright, valued, and needed. Indeed, they form the backbone of any social setting because there are more of them. But they're average, or routine—not remarkable.

Another way to define routine, or average, performance is "the best of the worst and the worst of the best." These performers are the best of the mediocre middle, neither hot nor cold but lukewarm. The problem is that average performance doesn't get you noticed. In the work world it doesn't lead to promotions or raises, and it doesn't create strong relationships and bonds. Average performance also doesn't transform people's lives. To do that, you want to achieve superlative, remarkable performance. You want to be among the best of the best.

The definition of "best," of course, is debatable, but most people agree when they see or experience something remarkable. As Supreme Court Justice Potter Stewart once said about pornography, "I know it when I see it." The same is true for "best" and "remarkable." Definitions may vary, but there's no mistaking it when we see it.

But there is a simple way to tell whether your performance is routine or remarkable: look for the Encore Effect—or the lack of it.

How can you see the Encore Effect in the workaday world that we all live in? Here are some examples:

	ROUTINE	REMARKABLE
Money	Your pay raises consist only of annual cost-of-living increases.	You are given raises when you ask for them. Better yet, you get raises without asking for them!
Responsibility	Your superiors ask you to take on more work of the same kind you're doing now.	Instead of asking you to take on *more* work, your superiors ask you to take on *more challenging* work.
Praise	You can't recall having been singled out for praise or given an award for your contribution.	Your contribution is consistently acknowledged and rewarded by your superiors.
Reviews	Your performance reviews are "average." You "get by."	You consistently receive above-average or superior reviews and are recommended for promotions.

	ROUTINE	REMARKABLE
Peers	You feel more valued for your personality or longevity than your performance.	Your coworkers and peers look to you for leadership, guidance, counsel, and help. You're the "go-to" person in your shop.
"Fight-For" Factor	When you decide to change jobs or leave the workforce, no one fights to change your mind.	Your manager works hard to make sure you are happy and rewarded so you won't leave. If you do decide to change jobs, your superiors and peers fight to change your mind.
Service	Competent and/or courteous.	Exceptional and enthusiastic.

Bad performances get talked about—but for the wrong reasons. An average performance gets overlooked and forgotten. Exceptional performances get talked about for the right reasons. Routine gets the job done. Remarkable gets it done and leaves the impression that there's a whole lot more where that came from. My own definition of a remarkable performance is one that is so unique and valued that people notice and tell others about it.

Remarkable Performances

There are more people who would like to be a star athlete than those who would be willing to invest what it takes to become one. It is fun to *be* a star in your field, but the process of *becoming* a star is difficult and requires hard work, often over a long period of time.

Here's an example. In 1999 Barrington Irving was a fifteen-year-old Jamaican American living in inner-city Miami. Like most of his peers, he saw little future for himself outside of an athletic scholarship to college. But a chance meeting with a Jamaican airline pilot led to an invitation to see the cockpit of the Boeing 777 the pilot flew for United Airlines.

Barrington Irving fell in love with flying. For the next eight years he ate, drank, slept, and dreamed aviation. He helped to wash planes at the airport to make money for flight lessons. He spent hours "flying" a $40 flight simulator on his family's home computer. He turned down football scholarships to enroll in a local community college to begin working toward a degree in aviation.

Over the years he earned his private, commercial pilot, and flight instructor licenses as well as earning an instrument rating. But he had no plane. So, in 2003, he contacted airplane component manufacturers and asked if they would donate components to him so he could have a plane built. Columbia, an aircraft manufacturer, agreed to assemble the plane if he could furnish the parts.

One year and $300,000 worth of donated components later, Irving had his plane: a Columbia 400 named *Inspiration*, one of the world's fastest single-engine airplanes. He was ready to fulfill his dream of becoming the first person of African descent, and the youngest person ever, to fly solo around the globe. On March 23, 2007, at age twenty-three, he climbed into his plane and taxied down the runway. He returned to Miami 26,800 miles and 95 days later, after setting two world records.

Irving went on to found Experience Aviation, Inc., a nonprofit organization that encourages young people to consider careers in aviation and aerospace. Grants from the Miami-Dade Empowerment Trust and donations of computers and software from Microsoft led to the establishment of the Experience Aviation Learning Center at Miami's Opa-locka Airport.

Barrington Irving is a remarkable young man. And his round-the-world flight was a remarkable achievement. The performance made the news. But think how many smaller remarkable performances he put in that led him to the one that would make him famous. Moreover, on his round-the-world trips, he could have thrown in the towel and given up at any point along the way. Fear, homesickness, boredom, and obstacles of every variety plagued him during the flight. He was under no obligation to continue—other than to achieve the goal he had set for himself and honor his commitment to those who had helped him.

Irving did more than just *aspire* to the remarkable: he worked hard to achieve it. And it all started because he had a passion for flying and because, at the age of fifteen, he decided that the routine of inner-city life was not what he wanted as his future. He saw an opportunity for a *remarkable* life, and he grabbed it. And once he grabbed it, he refused to let go.

Achieving the Remarkable

Do you dream of achieving more than the ordinary in life?

Then do it!

So how do you get started? Try this. Do the important jobs or tasks you have to perform before turning out the light tonight remarkably—even if you're alone, even if there is no one there to watch you. After all, you will still be aware of how you do what you need to do. Remember: self-respect is the first step toward gaining the respect of others. Ask more of yourself today; it will lead others to expect more of you tomorrow.

CHAPTER 3

WHY REMARKABLE
PERFORMANCE MATTERS

Denver, Colorado, near where I live, is a huge sports city. With four pro teams in town—the Denver Nuggets (basketball), Colorado Avalanche (hockey), Denver Broncos (football), and Colorado Rockies (baseball)—it's difficult not to overhear a sports discussion wherever you go. And the tenor and tone of the discussions depend on how the teams are faring. Let's face it—sports fans love winners.

For instance, in 2007 the buzz about the Rockies was tepid after they got off to a lackluster start. But whoa!—after winning twenty-one of their last twenty-two games, the Rockies faced the Boston Red Sox in the World Series.

The Broncos are the veterans of the Denver sports scene. The years when John Elway was quarterback made Mile High Stadium a shrine to excellence until the team moved to a new stadium in 2001. But the natives were restless in 2007. The team finished with a 7–9 record and on October 7 suffered a humiliating 41–3 drubbing at the hands of their longtime rivals, the San Diego Chargers. A rarity in Bronco history, the fans started filing out of the stadium before that game even finished.

Sports fans love to back winners. When their teams are giving encore-producing performances, the fans fill the seats. Witness the remarkable performance by the New England Patriots: 16–0 in the regular season. An undefeated regular season goes a long way toward selling out next season's games.

But most sports fans—like fans everywhere, whether you're in the arts or in sales—are fair-weather friends. Yes, your mother and your spouse may be committed to you through thick and thin, but the public isn't. It doesn't take many lackluster performances before they're ready to file out at halftime.

My point? Performance counts. If you want to win the loyalty of your customers, coworkers, boss, and other constituents, you need to turn in a consistently strong performance. And if you want to wow them, you need to turn in a remarkable performance.

Every Day Is Game Day

My friend Julie encountered a remarkable performance at an Au Bon Pain where she went for dinner in the Newark airport.

After her order was taken, she noticed four women behind the counter singing and dancing as they made the sandwiches.

"Their behavior had all the customers smiling." So Julie asked the woman who was making her sandwich, who seemed to be the leader of this culinary choir, what motivated her to look at her job so positively.

"I tell these ladies every day that each order they make is a chance to do something special for someone and to love what they do because you never know where this job may lead you."

Julie was so impressed by the woman's performance that she now goes back to that Au Bon Pain every time she has a stopover in Newark.

When you work with people, whether customers, clients, or coworkers, every day is game day. Every interaction is an opportunity to give a remarkable performance. The thing is, whether we realize it or not, we all perform for others in one way or another. Disney World knows this—at Disney theme parks employees are called "cast members," and every potential interaction with a "guest" is defined as being onstage (as opposed to backstage).

A Remarkable Performance Can Take Place in an Instant

Some people deliver remarkable performances over and over, throughout the day. Take the physician who sees fifty patients over the course of a day and is just as caring and thorough with his last patient as he is with the first. He probably also has a six-month waiting list for new-patient appointments as a result. Or the legal assistant who supports two attorneys and three para-legals in a high-pressure boutique law firm and is always one step ahead of them all. She seems to anticipate every need, putting out fires before they have a chance to spiral out of control. And she does it with grace and cheerfulness. She is exactly the sort of employee who gets weekly calls from legal headhunters trying to hire her away.

For people like this, every moment is an opportunity to shine.

Let me tell you about a school bus driver in Kentucky. After returning to the bus yard after the day's runs, he received a lot of good-natured ribbing from the other drivers because he wasn't wearing a coat on what was a freezing day.

The bus driver smiled and took it in stride. But later a school administrator joined the group. When he asked the driver why he hadn't worn his coat that day, the real story came out. He had driven a class on a field trip, and a student on his bus didn't have a coat. So he had given it to the student. The driver hadn't forgotten his coat at all. He was just taking care of one of his "customers" at his own expense.

A lot of remarkable performances occur every day that never make the front page of the newspapers. Often, it's because the performers are bus drivers and other people who don't perform at Carnegie Hall.

A remarkable performance is the antithesis of "just getting by." Nobody would have remembered the bus driver that day if he hadn't given his coat to a student in need. What made his performance remarkable was that he did.

Remarkable Performances Can Be Life-Changing

Born almost totally deaf, Stephen Hopson overcame tremendous obstacles to become a highly successful stockbroker for

Merrill Lynch. He's also a published author, a motivational speaker, and the first deaf person to earn his instrument rating as a pilot. (His rating requires him to fly with a copilot who can handle the radio for him.) I have gotten to know Stephen through our mutual love of flying.

Stephen's life was changed in a single moment by a larger-than-life elementary school teacher. One day she asked the class a question, and Stephen raised his hand, secretly hoping she wouldn't call on him. But she did, and Stephen stammered out the answer. "That's right, Stephen!" she exclaimed approvingly.

That simple act of approval by someone Stephen respected and admired made a powerful and lasting impression on him. Decades later he describes it as life-changing. Most likely the teacher had no idea what a powerful impact her words had, even years later. Undoubtedly her remarkable performances in the classroom throughout the school year had prepared the ground by winning Stephen's affection and admiration to begin with.

We never know when a few simple words—or simple acts—will make a powerful and positive difference. There are no time-outs when it comes to our performance in life. All it takes is an instant to touch someone—or to undermine a lifetime of good performances.

Your Performance Is Telling

Branding is a hot topic today. A great brand can't be bought—it can only be earned through ingenuity and hard work. Done right, a good brand is priceless. That is why more and more individuals have become interested in "personal branding."

I define a brand as a promise for the future based on past performance. Ranchers used to burn their brands into the flanks of their cattle. It was a permanent mark that established identity and possession and separated one steer from another. Its value was that it was instantly recognizable. The same is true of products today. Think of the Coca-Cola logo, the golden arches of McDonald's, and Apple's logo of an apple with a bite missing. When a brand has a strong identity, there is no mistaking what it represents.

An organization's brand is, in large part, the cumulative impact of the individuals who work there. Remarkable employees who are committed and capable add to it; apathetic or incompetent employees subtract from it. It's simple math.

An encore brand, whether personal or organizational, demonstrates a great deal about the person or the organization. It tells us about:

1. Commitment

Commitment is the price you are willing to pay to get remarkable results.

Performance, on the other hand, reveals the price you have paid already.

When we deliver a remarkable performance, we are saying in effect, "There is no other place or person I would rather spend my 'commitment' on than you." And when we deliver a poor performance, we convey the opposite message—that we'd rather spend our commitment elsewhere.

Realistically, commitment is not an either/or decision. We make choices every day that reveal different levels of commit-

ment. For instance, I enjoy a good movie, but I have no intention of going into the movie business. My commitment to good
cinema has limits.

It is fine to set limits on our commitment and engagements—
we all have to make such choices daily. The challenge is to com-
mit ourselves to the things that matter to us the most.

If I were to break down the levels of commitment we experience, it might look like this:

Interested	Interested individuals are curious enough to focus their attention on an area of interest. Their behavior is the equivalent of flipping through magazines or listening to *CNN Headline News* while working out at the gym—it rarely leads to remarkable or exceptional performance.
Informed	Those who consistently focus their attention are those who learn. This level of commitment results in persistent, intentional study and is the foundation, but not the end, of remarkable performance. Informed individuals subscribe to magazines, buy books, take classes, attend seminars, and make it a point to talk to other informed individuals.
Involved	Those who use what they learn and apply it diligently to their careers and lives are involved individuals. They don't just talk a good talk—they're playing the game.
Immersed	To become an expert or specialist in a chosen field requires study and application to a greater degree than most people are willing to undertake. Immersed individuals surround themselves with their craft and practice it continually. They

look at the world through eyes focused by their passion for the subject. This is the gateway to remarkable performance; such individuals rise above the pack and stand out in the crowd.

Invested | Those who are recognized as leaders in their field are invested individuals. They give consistently remarkable performances because they have invested more time, talent, experience, and resources to improve whatever it is they are working on.

Innovative | True leaders in any field go beyond the norm to break new ground through innovation. They become the example of what is possible, and they are always changing the game in positive ways. Innovative individuals are those who exemplify remarkable performance; they set new standards of excellence and remarkable performance.

The closer you are to "innovative" in your performance, the more recognizable your encore brand—you!—becomes as representing someone who is consistently dependable and indispensable in your field.

The next thing performance tells us about is:

2. *Professionalism*

When I first met Fred the postman (the real-life postal carrier Fred Shea, who formed the basis of my book *The Fred Factor*), I realized that he was more worried about my mail than I was. I've come to believe that this is the hallmark of a remarkable performance by someone who is a thorough professional.

What do I mean by a "professional"? The professional is someone who worries more about the impact of his or her performance on you than you do. The professional is more worried about your problems (as they relate to his or her product or service) than you are. In essence, your problems and opportunities become those of the professionals, who do their best even when they don't have time or feel at their best. That kind of remarkable performance is not the result of an impulse that occurs only when conditions are perfect. It comes about because the professional works to create the right conditions and to overcome any obstacles.

When you realize you are in the hands of a professional, you can relax. You know that your concerns will be addressed and that the professional will take care of you. And that is the feeling of confidence that *you* want to inspire in others.

Encore performances do a better job than anything else in demonstrating:

3. Skills

One of the highest compliments I receive is to be approached by an individual after a speech and told that he or she wants to be a professional speaker too. The individual has watched my performance and come to the conclusion that he or she can do what I do. Why am I flattered? Because evidently I made it look easy. And making the difficult look easy is a sign of mastery in any profession.

Performance, of course, is ultimately not about thinking or

knowing but about doing. Even those who get paid to think for a living, such as consultants and other knowledge experts, must be able to communicate their ideas in a compelling and convincing manner. Performance is about more than what we know; it's about what we *do* with what we know.

To do anything adequately requires basic skills. The encore performer has gone far beyond the rudimentary to hone his or her skills to a high level. Encore performers demonstrate that they know how to do what they do, that they've practiced and perfected what they do, and that they still have a commitment to becoming better.

Mastering basic skills is critically important to being able to solve problems and seize opportunities. A recent issue of *Portfolio* magazine profiled the world's top ten inventors (as determined by the most U.S. patents awarded). Many of the inventors held doctorates in science and engineering. But none of them cited their degree as critical to their success. Rather, most of them started by identifying a problem (or opportunity, depending on how you frame it) and then trying to come up with a solution. Leonard Forbes, number six on the list (671 patents awarded), says, "I look for something not being done efficiently. I tour around a lot of conferences and keep up on the literature to try to identify problems. It's not usually an 'aha' moment, but more a process of elimination."

To be a remarkable performer, think about things that are not being done efficiently or profitably or well in your workplace or industry or community. Can you suggest a solution to the problem? Are you able to spot opportunities that others can't?

Remarkable performers don't wait for problems and opportunities to come to them—they actively look for problems and opportunities.

What else can you tell from someone's performance? How about their . . .

4. Values

Values are those beliefs that a person holds most dear. Over time, that which we hold most dear becomes what we are known for.

The founder of the Chick-Fil-A restaurant chain, Truett Cathy, is a proactive Christian who believes that Sunday should be a day of rest for employees and families. As a result, all of the 1,240 restaurants in the chain are closed on Sundays, Thanksgiving Day, and Christmas Day. Closing its restaurants one day a week costs Chick-Fil-A revenues—but it is a vivid example of the company's values and has become part of its brand.

Victor Portillo is operations director for a six-store Domino's Pizza franchise in Texas. Averaging 150 miles a day on the road, he carries a portable air compressor with him to help people who are stranded on the roadside with a flat tire. "I probably put it to use twice a month," he says. "I just really enjoy talking to the people I help, much like knocking on someone's door to deliver a pizza." Portillo's attitude and willingness to serve others extend far beyond roadside assistance. In 2005 he traveled to New Orleans to aid the Hurricane Katrina victims by handing out more than six thousand pizzas a week from a trailer.

Portillo's values affect everything he does. Think about how your own values affect your life, your job, and your interactions with others. Are your values reflected in your actions? If not, what can you do differently?

Every performer is known for something. Over time, your brand is a composite of the values you act on every day.

Someone's level of performance tells you a great deal about his or her commitment, professionalism, mastery of skills, and values. But there is one final clue you can get from someone's performance. It is subtle but telling. Performance is also about . . .

5. *Character*

I define integrity as the distance between your lips and your life. Your performance is a visible sign of your integrity and character. The opposite, of course, is insincerity. The word "insincere" comes from the Latin phrase that means "without wax." In the ancient world, unscrupulous pottery and sculpture dealers would hide flaws and cracks with wax, which worked well until the objects were heated and the wax melted. *Sine cere*—a character trait that suggests no hidden flaws or motives—is the basis of the English word "sincerity."

Integrity, sincerity, honesty, and transparency are all character traits of remarkable performers. The word "hypocrite," on the other hand, comes from the Greek word *hupokrites*, which means "actor," or "one who plays a part." Remarkable performers don't play parts—they don't try to be someone they are not. Their commitment drives them to become the very best of *who they are*.

Remarkable performers have consistent values.

In my experience, these are the qualities shared by remarkable performers—by those who excel. People who consistently perform at the peak of their abilities attract our attention and gain our trust.

Remember this: performance matters. It is telling. People recognize a remarkable performance when it occurs, but they also recognize what it means about the performer. Think about what your win-loss record looks like in your career and in your personal life. Each one of us has complete control over what we do to keep our "fans" coming back for more.

CHAPTER 4

A DIFFERENT KIND
OF PDA

When employees of various-sized companies were asked in a *BusinessWeek* magazine poll, "Are you one of the top 10 percent of performers in your company?" an overwhelming number said yes. In fact, overall, 90 percent replied affirmatively; among executives the percentage was 97 percent.

In other words, nearly everyone thinks they perform at the top of their game. At the very least, no one can say we're lacking in self-confidence!

But is this really a true representation of our performance?

Obviously, 90 percent or more of us can't be among the top 10 percent of all employees. Clearly, a lot of people do not know how they are really doing. Wishful thinking alone won't help you get ahead in today's world. You need to demonstrate it with your performance.

Making the Complex Simple

Albert Einstein, with his theory of relativity, dealt with some of the most complex ideas ever formulated about how our universe works. And yet he was able to reduce these complex ideas down to one of the simplest formulas ever devised: $E = mc^2$— energy equals mass times the speed of light squared. Whether or not we genuinely understand the math behind it, the point is that Einstein's equation reduces something incredibly complex down to several fundamental components. With study, anyone can learn and understand the essence of the theory of relativity.

Although our universe is highly complex and complicated, it pales in comparison to the complexity of the human mind, will, and emotions. Just think about your own life. You have thousands of thoughts, impulses, and emotions and perform thousands of actions every day. Your mind contains a record of everything you've ever seen, done, or said; the synapses in your brain are firing all day long like the spark plugs in a NASCAR engine at Daytona.

Our challenge is to get our arms around all that complexity and to focus it toward goals that bring us satisfaction and achievement. People who fail to harness their minds are living their lives at the beck and call of their impulses and taking directions from others.

Like Einstein, we need to find a way to reduce the complexity of human variables and apply them to the goal of remarkable performance. We need a formula. And that is what I want to pass on to you in this chapter. For there is such a formula. I describe it as: P + D + A = RP, where P = Passion, D = Discipline, A = Action, and RP stands for Remarkable Performance.

I call this formulation the Performance Development Agenda, or PDA.

Formulas like the one I'm suggesting are not panaceas; they are a way to simplify the complex and make it understandable. I'm not suggesting that the PDA formula is going to change your life, at least not overnight. But I do think it can become a useful mental road map or compass that you can use to evaluate your choices and determine the actions and directions you're going to take. Let's look more closely at each of the PDA elements: passion, discipline, and action.

Passion

I am going to address passion in more depth in the next chapter. For now, think of its place in the PDA formula: it comes *first*. Passion is where life begins. Consider the following quote.

> *I want to die at a hundred years old with an American flag on my back and the star of Texas on my helmet, after screaming down an Alpine descent on a bicycle at 75 miles per hour. I want to cross one last finish line as my stud wife and my ten children applaud, and then I want to lie down in a field of those famous French sunflowers and gracefully expire: the perfect contradiction to my once anticipated poignant early demise.*

Who said that? If you guessed Lance Armstrong, the only man in history to win the three-week-long Tour de France bicycle race seven times (*in a row*), you're right. And the "once-anticipated poignant early demise" he mentions? Testicular cancer at age twenty-five, resulting in brain surgery and chemotherapy—from which he not only recovered but went on to become a Tour de France champion.

As a cyclist, Lance Armstrong is the personification of passion. And since his cancer recovery, he has become just as passionate about cancer research, raising millions of dollars through his foundation, lobbying Congress, and encouraging cancer victims the world over.

Encounters with passionate people are memorable. You are captivated not only by what they do but by the way they do it. You may not agree with them, but there's no doubt about what they believe is important.

What are you passionate about? Lance Armstrong discovered his passion as a teenager. Not all of us discover our passion that early in life. Indeed, some people don't discover it until middle age or later.

To discover what you are passionate about, ask yourself: *What would I like to spend the rest of my life doing?* I'm convinced that how you answer that question will lead you to your true passion. And I also believe that everybody has one. You should never give up trying to find that passion and then pursuing it, whatever the financial benefits or consequences. As Marsha Sinetar titled her 1989 best-seller: *Do What You Love, the Money Will Follow.*

Discipline

Passion is the fuel that drives performance. But without discipline, passion is just loud talk and noise. Or as they say in Texas, "All hat and no cattle." Passionate people who lack discipline will end up in life exactly where they began. They may be pedaling furiously, but they're stuck in first gear.

Delivering remarkable performance requires consistent and persistent effort. That's why discipline is critical. When discipline is lacking, results are inconsistent and sporadic. It is discipline that enables us to do what needs to be done even when we are not at our best.

In the PDA formula, it is discipline that turns passion into action. A 2,000-horsepower engine will move a dragster exactly nowhere if it does not engage the transmission. The most passionate person in the world will achieve little without discipline.

Let me give you an example of discipline, drawing once again on the career of Lance Armstrong.

In a DVD entitled *Road to Paris*, we follow Armstrong's U.S. Postal Service team as they prepare for the 2001 Tour de France. An added feature of the DVD gives a glimpse into his personal training regimen. It's the dead of winter, and he's doing reconnaissance rides on his bike in the French Alps. A team car driven by the team director, Johan Bruyneel, is pacing Armstrong up a foggy, wet, freezing mountain road. At a point where an avalanche has blocked the road, they stop for Armstrong to eat. (He would spend six-plus hours a day on the bike when training.) Lance tells Johan, "I still want to ride a little more, you know?" So Johan suggests that Lance do another ten kilometers down the mountain. Lance pauses a moment and then says:

"I'll go down ten [kilometers], then come back [up]."

As Armstrong pedals off into the fog, Bruyneel turns to the team mechanic and says, "That's what it takes to win the Tour. Training in this weather. Nobody sees that."

The DVD opens with this quote:

> *If you wish to be out front,*
> *Then act as if you were behind.*

> —LAO-TZU, SIXTH CENTURY B.C.

Nothing better defines Lance Armstrong's attitude toward life—and that of virtually all other remarkable performers. It's the things we do over and over again, often behind the scenes, that ultimately result in remarkable performances. It is the discipline we bring to our efforts. Ask yourself:

- How many times did I rehearse and refine my sales presentation before giving it?

- How many books did I read (and re-read) about my industry/career/service/skills?

- How much time do I spend each day in the gym, and how many days each week, to keep myself physically fit?

- How many thank-you notes and follow up e-mails do I send to important customers, clients, volunteers, or friends?

- How much of my income do I invest in myself to further my vocation and my passion?

- How much space do I make in my schedule to do the things that matter to me the most, whether developing my skills, spending time with my family, or giving back to my congregation or community?

Action

Action is where the rubber meets the road in our lives. If there's one message to take away from this chapter above any other, it is this: don't confuse activity with action.

You can think the *right thoughts* all day long, but even if those thoughts make you feel good, nothing happens until you take *action*. The difference between a mediocre performance and a remarkable one is usually the difference between what you know and what you do with what you know.

Let me give you an example. When downloading a vendor-mandated software upgrade to my desktop computer recently, my computer froze. It was put out of business for several days. So I began the frustrating process of communicating with the software company's tech support folks—eight of them by the time I was done—first by e-mail, using my laptop, and then by phone. They all offered advice on what I should do, but none of it worked. A lot of heat was generated by their input and activity, but no light.

Out of desperation, I finally spent $250 to have a computer consultant come to my office to fix my computer. In the end, I spent three times the cost of the software upgrade to fix the problem that the upgrade caused.

My point? There is a big difference between activity and action. Right action creates a solution or an outcome; simple activity is an attempt or an input. All the activity of the tech support reps accomplished nothing. Activity is effort without effect. Action is what achieves a desired outcome.

Some people hide behind activity and use it as an excuse to absolve themselves of responsibility ("I'm so busy!").

Remarkable performers focus on the outcome they're striving to achieve and say no to any activity that would divert their efforts. They know exactly where they are going, and they focus on how to get there.

PDA and Performance

With the proverbial three-legged stool, you need all three legs to stay upright. One weak leg will land you on your butt in a hurry. The same is true of the PDA formula. Every leg of performance—passion and discipline and action—is critical.

> Passion and discipline *without action* is just daydreaming.
> Discipline and action *without passion* is a fire made from damp wood that quickly goes out.
> Action and passion *without discipline* is a race car without a driver.

It takes all three elements to create remarkable performances—over and over and over again.

PART TWO

Achieving
the
Encore Effect

CHAPTER 5

PASSION:
THE FUEL FOR
REMARKABLE PERFORMANCE

John Wesley was the cofounder of what ultimately became the Methodist Church. Considered a controversial maverick, Wesley was forbidden by the Anglican Church to preach from its pulpits. So, instead, he would ride out into the countryside, pick a spot in an open field, and begin to preach. John Wesley gave such remarkable performances that before long large crowds would gather to hear him, and he gained such notoriety that listeners wanted to hear more of what he had to say.

Someone once asked Wesley how he was able to attract such large crowds with his preaching. Wesley responded, "I simply set myself on fire and people come to watch me burn."

That's *passion*.

Set Yourself on Fire

Remarkable performance isn't just about what we do; it's also about how we do it. Passion is the fuel that lets us "set ourselves on fire."

If you are going to get the marketplace excited about your brand—about you—you have to get people excited about who you are and what you do. I'll show you how in the chapters ahead.

Remember: *No one will be more passionate about your performance than you are yourself.*

The good news is that passion can be created and stoked. It's up to you to do so.

Pizza and Passion

"You've just got to meet her!" people say about Heather Conrad. Heather is a trainer for a Domino's Pizza franchise based in Staunton, Virginia. What makes her remarkable is how she's able to bring out the best in others.

"People typically do not see what they're capable of," Heather says. "My job is to grow people, to help them accomplish something others thought not possible." How does she do this? Just like any remarkable developer of people, she is able to see more possibility and potential in people than they sometimes are able to see in themselves.

An ordinary performer would typically train new hires in their duties and help develop the skills of more seasoned employees. Heather does that, of course, but she goes further. She's a mentor and a motivator to those she works with, helping to instill pride and ambition in all Domino's employees. As she says, "My job is about growing people and enabling my team to grow. It's about being big on the inside."

Heather doesn't just show her team that they can be better than they imagined—she shows them how to do it. Her personal attention and enthusiasm for their success doesn't *drive* them— it *pulls* them toward achieving their potential. Nobody likes to be driven by someone else; it feels like being pushed. But when someone can show us how to be bigger on the inside—in our attitude and mind-set—that can help attract or pull us toward what we can become.

We too can become "big on the inside" in how we define our work and the passion we bring to it.

I've come to believe that life isn't just about living out our passions but about living passionately. The difference is subtle, but important. Let me explain.

A close friend of mine asked for my help. He hadn't been able to identify his purpose in life. He was successful in his personal and professional lives—he was a speaker who had built a successful direct selling organization and created a very effective nonprofit organization that ministered to young people—yet he couldn't find that "one thing" that he considered to be his life's purpose.

I wasn't able to help him find his singular and unique purpose that day. That is something he is going to have to discover for himself. But I was able to give him a piece of advice: *Until you find your purpose, continue to do things purposefully, with energy and intention.* When you do things purposefully, with energy and intention, sometimes the purpose will emerge.

In the everyday world, most of us don't get to focus exclusively on doing those things we're passionate about. The solution? Do everything important with passion.

All too often people convince themselves that their dream job will never materialize. So they give up trying to find it and just go through the motions of the job they have already. The fact is, if you simply punch the clock and do just enough to get by in your present job, you may be able to keep your job, but that's about all you can hope for.

By doing your job with all the passion and enthusiasm and creativity and energy you have, you will make yourself increasingly valuable in the eyes of those around you. And as that happens, your opportunities will expand. When people are excited about you and about what you have to offer, the possibilities that will open up may surprise you.

Here's how it works:

> *Ability* determines what you *can* do.
> *Aptitude* determines what you can *learn* to do.
> *Aspiration* determines what you *hope* to do.
> *Attitude* determines what you *believe* you can do.
> But *passion* determines what you *want* to do!

Sure, there is a lot of gimmickry, fakery, and posturing in the world. But passion cannot be faked—at least not for long. It can, however, be nurtured, developed, and cultivated. And as it becomes part of who you are, it will also become one of the ways in which people identify you.

As a parent or spouse, as a volunteer in your church or community, as an employee making a sales call, teaching a class, or leading a company, bringing passion to what you do each day is an exercise in living fully and influencing others by your example. Your passion affects not only you but those around you, in the following ways:

Passion invigorates. Passion helps to drive your achievement clock. You'll find yourself waking up ready to get to the important work you believe in.

Passion inspires. It helps you aspire higher and see farther than those without it.

Passion sustains. Obstacles and difficulties become mere stepping-stones to success rather than stumbling blocks. Passion keeps you going after others give up.

Passion comforts. When you act with passion, you know that you have done your best, regardless of the outcome.

Passion initiates. It overcomes the inertia and enables you to push the boundaries of what's possible.

Passion completes. Because you begin only the work that is worthwhile, you become a consistent closer and finisher.

Passion enhances. It expands the value and benefits of the work being done.

The Four Insights of a Passionate Performer

1. Passionate people know for whom they are performing.

Every performance has an audience. Passionate people know their audience inside and out. They know exactly who will invite them back for a repeat performance. (Amazon.com founder and

CEO Jeff Bezos has said, "Don't fear your competitor—they'll never send you money. Fear your customer.")

Write down what you know about the main clients, customers, or VIPs in your life. You can perform remarkably for them only if you know what they consider "remarkable" to be.

2. *Passionate people know* how to perform remarkably.

Passionate people innovate, create, and change the way business is done. They are willing to break the rules. But to do that, they have to first know what the rules are.

What can you do differently in your performance in the next sixty days? Try to become known as the most innovative person in your group, on your floor, in your division, or throughout your company.

3. *Passionate people know* why they perform.

We all have myriad motives for doing the things we do: money, pride, prestige, acclaim, security, fear. Passionate people are driven by more powerful motives: their sense of self-worth, self-satisfaction, and self-fulfillment. As they begin meeting their personal expectations, they also meet the expectations of others.

Does someone else's approval mean more to you than your own? How would your passion increase if you were driven by self-worth and self-approval?

4. *Passionate people know* what their performance needs to look like.

A result that is off by an inch today will be off by a mile in the future. Passionate people understand their goals and objectives—and focus on meeting them. Many undesired results are the consequence of lack of focus.

When was the last time you asked your audience, "How would you define an encore performance?" What could you do to be a more supportive parent, spouse, or friend? How much more effective would you be if you knew what your family and friends need from you? You can go beyond satisfying your audience only when you know what they want.

Cultivating Passion

I believe passion can be developed and cultivated. Here are five things you can do to increase your passion over time.

1. Study and learn.

You can go a long way toward becoming a passionate performer by buying the best books, subscribing to the best magazines, and going to free university lectures through Apple's iTunes U (podcasts from MIT, Stanford, Duke, Berkeley, and other top universities). There is no shortage of ways to become an expert in your field—and grow more passionate in the process.

Surveys periodically tell us how many Americans are reading or not reading books, and the trends are not always encouraging, especially among young people. But since the advent of the Internet, book-reading statistics don't tell the whole story, since so many people read material online these days. Given the unlimited amounts of information available today, there is little justification for anyone not being a reader. Nor is there any reason for anyone to be unable to gain the information that would fuel his or her ascendancy to remarkable-performer status.

2. *Use small achievements or successes to fuel larger ones.*

Remarkable performances are like losing weight. Which goal sounds more achievable—losing one pound per week for a year or losing fifty-two pounds? The result may be the same, but psychologically these goals are as different as night and day. Focus on achieving a remarkable performance today, then another one tomorrow—not on becoming company CEO.

3. *Look to other passionate people as role models.*

Reach out to people you respect for their passion and performance. Start a group of like-minded people with similar goals. Avoid the people who act as "blockers." Remember, passion begets passion.

4. *Plug the leaks.*

Examine those areas in your life where your resources (your time, talent, and skills) are not being put to the best use. A student once asked Albert Einstein how many feet were in a mile; he replied that he didn't know. Seeing the student's amazement, Einstein replied, "I make it a rule not to clutter my mind with simple information that I can find in a book in five minutes." Don't spend time on things that diffuse your focus and do not advance your goals.

5. Make passion part of your life.

Where the head goes, the heart will follow. You may not *feel* passionate, but when you decide you are going to become a passionate person, you *will* become one. If you act the part and succeed in the part, one day you will discover that you have *become* the part! If you deliberately and consciously act with passion, you will come to feel that passion.

The Passion and the Purpose

John Wood was one of many thousands of "Microsoft millionaires"—employees made rich by the company's stock run-up in the 1990s. On an eighteen-day hiking trip through Nepal, he visited a school and discovered seventy-five kids crowded into a dirt-floored, one-room schoolroom without any textbooks. It was here that he discovered his true passion. He returned to America, founded a nonprofit organization called Room to Read, and eventually quit his job at Microsoft to focus his efforts on Room to Read. That organization has now distributed nearly 3 million books, constructed 287 schools, established 3,600 libraries, and funded more than 2,000 scholarships—all in needy Third World settings where kids were being left behind because of their lack of access to education.

John Wood's remarkable performance at Microsoft enabled him, in the end, to discover his true passion in life.

Wood discovered his passion serendipitously. John Robbins *uncovered* his passion. Heir to the Baskin-Robbins ice cream empire, Robbins, in reaction to the effects of a poor diet on his father, walked away from the business. He found his passion as a worldwide author and spokesman for healthy living based on a vegetarian lifestyle.

Remarkable performances require energy and effort. Remarkable men and women throughout history, like John Wesley, have known that passion is the fuel that gives them their life purpose and helps make them remarkable.

CHAPTER 6

PREPARATION: WHERE REMARKABLE PERFORMANCE BEGINS

My friend Jon was interviewing for an important job opportunity, and to ensure that he did a remarkable job he researched the person who would be doing the interview. Among the many things Jon learned was that the interviewer served on the board of a Christian school that his own children attended. Jon was not only encouraged to learn of these shared values and faith but now had a solid connection with the interviewer.

On the breakfast table of winners in any area of life, you'll always find a large serving of preparation.

Each of us is creating our future *right now*. Whether the future is five minutes from now or five years, it is determined by our preparation—or lack of it. As we go about our workday, we don't often give thought to the kind of future our actions are creating. And yet the future we experience depends on the preparations we make today.

As an old Chinese proverb says, "Dig the well before you are thirsty."

We receive a lot of advice on how to prepare for things that *might* happen (hurricanes, terrorist attacks, IRS audits, divorce, financial calamity, medical emergencies, economic downturns), as well as the things we expect to happen (taking the SAT test, getting married, raising children, retiring, passing the bar exam, preparing a résumé, interviewing for a new job). We also have access to advice on how to achieve the things we *hope* will happen (closing the sale, getting the job, receiving a raise, improving our golf game).

But there is a lot less information available on the extra effort that will enable you to perform remarkably and the preparation that will separate your performance from everyone else's. Sometimes the difference between remarkable and ordinary—between "Thanks for coming" and "When can you come back?"—is razor-thin.

In his book *Slaying the Dragon*, Olympic sprinter Michael Johnson, who set world records in the 200- and 400-meter sprints in 1996, wrote:

> *Success is found in much smaller portions than most*
> *people realize. A hundredth of a second here or sometimes*
> *a tenth there can determine the fastest man in the world.*
> *At times we live our lives on a paper-thin edge that barely*
> *separates greatness from mediocrity and success from*
> *failure.*

> *Life is often compared to a marathon, but I think it*
> *is more like being a sprinter: long stretches of hard work*
> *punctuated by brief moments in which we are given the*
> *opportunity to perform at our best.*

A lot of us assume that it's the long stretches of hard work that make the difference in our lives. But it is our willingness not only to engage in the long stretches but to do a little bit more—that is, to prepare diligently—that makes our performance remarkable.

Preparation Breeds Confidence

I entered my first public speaking contest at the age of ten. I was a member of a 4-H club, and we needed a representative. I figured, how hard could it be?

My speech lasted three minutes, and it was a total flop. I stammered and stuttered and said things I didn't intend to say and forgot some of what I did mean to say. I don't know if the audience was more bored or amused by my performance. I barely recall seeing them in the midst of my humiliation.

After my baptism by fire into the world of public speaking, I realized that I could throw in the towel or learn from experience. I definitely didn't gain any confidence from the experience, but I did gain a measure of resolve. I decided to keep speaking—to enter contests, give talks to civic groups, and take any other opportunity to speak in public—until I could speak well enough to win.

So I spoke—a lot. And a funny thing happened: the more I

prepared and the harder I practiced, the more confidence I gained. And the more confidence I gained, the better my performances became. In due time, speaking became *fun* for me.

Everyone is anxious before giving a speech. I'm no exception. It's a form of performance anxiety, and if you lack it you probably aren't taking the experience seriously. I'm not terrified, as I once was, or even nervous, in the typical sense. Why? I've developed confidence and *proficiency* as a result of the *preparation and practice* I've put in.

The link between preparation, practice, and proficiency applies to every kind of performance. It's found everywhere from parenting and software programming to pastoring and public relations.

You can't merely get "psyched up" to perform remarkably. You need to be adequately prepared as well. Any notion that you'll do well enough whether or not you're prepared is only wishful thinking.

The worlds of work, sports, and entertainment offer countless examples of people who are consistently prepared and as a result prosper and win, even when they don't have as much talent as others. These areas also offer plenty of examples of those who tried to get by on sheer talent and who tanked. It takes only a single bad performance to undermine a reputation, and it can take years to rebuild it. If you want to succeed, you have to prepare.

The confidence you need can only come from doing something again and again.

Have you ever witnessed jazz musicians take off on long improvisations? You've probably wondered how they do it. How can they compose music on the spot? They can do it because they know the musical scales and chords backwards and forwards; they know what notes will work in which key, and they've spent years practicing and improving.

I once attended a concert by a renowned concert organist. In the middle of a Bach performance, he forgot where he was in the piece. I recognized his dilemma because I knew the piece so well. Instead of panicking, however, he simply improvised Bach-like phrases at the keyboard, his fingers flying over the keys, until he refound his place and could continue on. The rest of the audience had no idea that he had briefly lost his way, not only because of the confidence he exuded but also because he knew the music so well that he could improvise a stretch of faux-Bach.

Thorough Preparation Creates Tremendous Performances

Legendary speaker and trainer Joel Weldon (known for "Success comes in cans, not cannots") says: "You prepare for what you love." The level of our preparation is a declaration of the value we place on our performance and our audience.

Let me give you an example. Two guys are planning an early Saturday morning fly-fishing trip. Bob has spent several weeknights getting his gear ready. He's put fresh line on his reel, checked his rod for cracks or damage, checked the line guides to make sure they're on tight, then disassembled the rod and stored it in its carrying pouch. He's checked his waders for leaks and his net for breaks or ravels in the cord, and he's tied several new flies suitable for the stream where they'll fish. Because he has to get up at 4:00 A.M. on Saturday morning, he lays out his clothes in the spare bedroom so as not to wake his wife: flannel shirt, ball cap, sunglasses, lip balm. He's packed a small cooler with food and stored it in the refrigerator. Bob couldn't be more prepared.

Saturday morning when he pulls up in front of Jim's house at five-thirty sharp, there are no lights on. Their trip together goes downhill from there.

Bob loves to fish, and his preparation shows it. Jim *says* he loves to fish, but his lack of preparation says otherwise. I would be surprised if Bob calls Jim again to suggest they go fishing.

The bottom line is this: our actions—our preparation—speak louder than our words when it comes to how much we love what we do.

I am often asked to speak to civic, church, nonprofit, or other groups on a pro bono basis. I spend no less time preparing for those engagements than I do for my paid speaking engagements.

Why? Because of my passion for speaking and my love for my audience. When I speak to a group of people, I am communicating the essence of who I am and what I believe. But more importantly, I am communicating how much I value the members of my audience.

Why prepare any differently, any less diligently, just because I'm not getting paid? Most of the time the audience doesn't know whether or not I'm getting paid. They're going to judge my performance based on what I bring to them, not on my fee.

Our preparation becomes apparent throughout a typical day. Our preparation—or lack of it—becomes clear to those who watch us perform. Consider your own performance:

- Before a meeting, presentation, or project, ask yourself how thoroughly you have prepared. For instance, do you have a backup laptop for the PowerPoint presentation? Have you anticipated the questions you'll be asked?

- If you have a date planned with someone special, have you thought about what you are going to wear? Have you made dinner reservations? Have you bought the necessary tickets and cleaned the car?

- If you're a salesperson scheduled to meet with a prospective client, what have you done to prepare? Have you researched the client's company thoroughly? Are you aware of its needs and goals? Have you planned and rehearsed your presentation? Have you anticipated possible questions?

- If you're a manager giving an employee a performance review, have you reviewed the notes you've kept on his or her performance over the last year? Have you thought through what you want to say? Have you taken notes so that you can point to specific examples of the employee's performance for commendation or correction? Have you created a development plan for the employee?

In the past few pages, I've talked about your "audience" quite a bit. But the fact is that we all address different audiences every day, ranging from our families to those we work with in our jobs to the people we come across in our volunteer work. What do you want your audience to believe about how you feel about them and your relationship to them? Let your preparation do the talking.

Think about what it is you are getting ready to do—a corporate presentation, a sales call, an employee review, a family outing. Now picture in your mind what it would look like if it totally failed. Next, mentally go through the wreckage looking for what happened and why. This exercise will help you to anticipate potential problems and allow you to solve them in advance. This kind of preparation is planning-in-reverse: by anticipating the possibility of your computer dying in the midst of your sales presentation, you realize ahead of time that you need to have a backup on hand.

By projecting all the things that might go wrong, you can prepare for much of the "bad luck" that might befall you.

The Crucial 5 Percent

I like to think of preparation as the process of finding and seizing "the Crucial 5 Percent"—the extra 5 percent effort that no one else will be able to match.

Remember my discussion of the bell-shaped curve in chapter 2? The crucial 5 percent of preparation and performance is found out on the farther edge of that curve—where the curve flattens out and meets the horizontal. That's where the remarkable performers are to be found. Make it your goal to move out of the bulbous center of the bell shape—the heart of the average—and into that 5 percent at the extreme edge of the curve.

How do you do that?

1. Find out things about your "audience" that they won't imagine you could know, things that your competitors are unlikely to discover.

2. Anticipate every question that your audience might raise and formulate a strong answer. If you're willing to take a little risk, come up with a clever (but not flip) and memorable answer.

3. Rehearse every problem that might arise. For example, if you're making a presentation, practice unplugging your laptop and hooking up your backup to the projector. Anticipate what you will do if there is a power failure, or if your transportation breaks down.

4. Know more about your competitors' products, features, and benefits than they know themselves.

5. Become the expert in your field.

6. Through your appearance and demeanor, give your performance a level of gravitas that your audience will not forget.

7. Give your audience more than one reason to invite you back for a repeat performance.

There isn't room at the top for very many. Only so many encores will be called for. If you prepare today for a remarkable performance, you will be an encore waiting to happen.

CHAPTER 7

PRACTICE:
IT WON'T MAKE YOU PERFECT,
BUT IT WILL
MAKE YOU BETTER

According to *Golf Digest*, the odds of hitting a hole-in-one are about one in thirteen thousand. Don LeGate is ninety-eight years old, and he's shot seventeen holes-in-one. That could explain his nickname, "the Maestro." He lost his sight a few years ago, but he decided that wasn't going to prevent him from playing the game he loves. Now he's working on knocking in his eighteenth hole-in-one.

You too can become a remarkable performer like the Maestro. All it takes is practice.

The Circle of Fear

The Eagles call it "the circle of fear."

The Eagles, of course, are one of the top five best-selling musical acts of all time. In fact, their album *Greatest Hits 1971–1975* is the best-selling album in American history.

So what does the circle of fear have to do with a world-famous band? One word: practice. In the circle of fear, the four musicians arrange their chairs in a tight circle. With knees and guitars almost touching, they practice the complex harmonies that have made them famous. They sing them over and over again until they get them right.

They call it the circle of fear because, as band founder Glenn Frey explains, "There's nowhere to hide. You like to kinda come out here and see that everybody's got it and we're all, you know, singing the right things."

Remarkable performers don't practice to become perfect, but to become better. In fact, most people at the top of their game—whether it's music, sports, business, parenting, or charity—have spent years honing their skills and practicing their craft.

The circle of fear is really about how to profit from practice.

Did you start the workday practicing your job? (I'm guessing no.) Did you set aside time to practice the skills on which your livelihood depends? (Between getting the kids' homework done, preparing and eating dinner, cleaning up, and so forth, again, I'm guessing the answer is no.)

Let's face it: "practice" sounds like something artists, athletes, and actors do—not people in the everyday work world. Very few people in the world of work practice. The closest they come to it is a kind of "practice in process," based on the hope that the longer they do their job, the better they'll get at it. And if they're lucky, practice in process does help.

But to become a remarkable performer, you've got to learn a more disciplined way to practice. Instead of only practicing in process, you also need to learn to practice prior to performing. Both types of practice are necessary to be remarkable.

Ask any artist or athlete: practice is the key to performing well. Without it, your performing days—not to mention your encores and callbacks—may be numbered.

Deliberate Practice

What the Eagles call the circle of fear modern performance researchers call "deliberate practice." Geoffrey Colvin, a researcher and senior editor at *Fortune* magazine, differentiates between practice and deliberate practice: "Simply hitting a bucket of balls is not deliberate practice, which is why most golfers don't get better. Hitting an eight-iron three hundred times with a goal of leaving the ball within twenty feet of the pin 80 percent of the time, continually observing results and making appropriate adjustments, and doing that for hours every day—that's deliberate practice."

With that image in mind, it's not hard to figure out why the group at the top of a field is small. A *Fortune* study of twenty-year-old violinists divided the musicians into three groups: those who were good, those who were better, and those who were the best, as judged by music conservatory teachers. Those judged "best" had averaged ten thousand hours of deliberate practice since taking up the violin. Those judged "better" had averaged seventy-five hundred hours. And those judged "good" had averaged five thousand hours.

There are no perfect violinists—or salespeople, executives, teachers, or parents for that matter. But deliberate practice is what distinguishes those who excel from those who get by.

The fact is that *no matter how good you become, you can always get better.* And that's a good thing. It keeps work and life interesting and challenging, because if you had become as good as you would ever get, the balance of your days would be pretty monotonous.

Ten Minutes and Ten Years

The great thing about practice is that even a little bit of practice can result in demonstrable improvement. Given that few people in business practice at all, think about the difference that ten minutes of practice a day on your performance would make. A little investment can yield a big payoff. In fact, the connection between practice and remarkable performance is so well established that it has given rise to the "ten-year rule." It generally takes a decade (give or take) to reach what is considered a world-class performance. As researchers John Horn and Hiromi Masunaga put it: "The ten-year rule represents a very rough estimate, and most researchers regard it as a minimum, not an average."

Look at these top performers in terms of the ten-year rule: Tiger Woods began to play golf at age eighteen months, Bobby Fischer studied chess for nine years before becoming a grandmaster at age sixteen, Yo-Yo Ma took up the cello at age four, and Warren Buffett spent decades studying corporate financial statements to find companies in which to invest.

It may seem to take a very long time to become world-class. But don't be discouraged. It is achieved minute by minute and day by day. Practice deliberately for a set amount of time every day. Ten minutes, half an hour. Just recognize that it will probably take ten years to become *world-class*.

One of my earliest mentors, drawing on a metaphor about mastery, told me to rob a few gas stations on my way to the bank heist. He wasn't encouraging a life of crime. He was illustrating an important concept: to get remarkable at the big performances, practice getting good in the small performances along the way.

Learn to Practice and Practice to Learn

Deliberate practice means incorporating new insights and understanding as you practice daily. In other words, deliberate practice requires learning and building on the fruits of that learning.

Here are five ways to learn that can be applied by anyone who is striving to become a remarkable performer:

1. Think.

Someone once said that if the devil can't make you bad, he'll make you busy. Often, busyness prevents remarkable performances. If you're too busy to think about how you are currently performing, you'll be too busy to make the changes necessary to become better.

What performance do you want to improve? Think about what you've learned in the past: What works? What works best? What do you need to improve? What knowledge or skills do you need to take you to the next level? How could you improve your performance? What could you add, subtract, or do differently to make your performance remarkable?

2. *Observe*.

A new student began his studies by reporting to his professor, Louis Agassiz, the nineteenth-century Swiss-American naturalist and scientist. Agassiz took a fish from a jar and told the student to observe all he could about the fish and prepare a report on what he learned. After half an hour, the student felt that he had seen all there was to see, but he could not find the professor to report his findings. Out of boredom, the student went back and began to count the fish's scales and the spines on its fins and to sketch the fish, whereupon he made other discoveries. When Agassiz returned and received the student's report, he told the student to return to the fish and keep looking—for three whole days. Years later, when the student had achieved his own prominence in the field, he described his experience with Agassiz as the best zoological lesson he'd ever been given.

What the student learned was the difference between looking and observing. Every waking moment we see people, places, things, and actions. But how many of them do we observe for the purpose of learning from them?

Years ago I spent a day with Ron Arden, one of the top speech coaches in the world. I'd sent Ron an hour-long video of my presentation in advance. I assumed we'd work our way through the video over the course of the day. After eight intensive hours packed with insights and ideas, we'd reviewed only eight minutes of the video. What made Ron such a remarkable coach was that he didn't just look at my tape—he observed me and my performance.

When you have the opportunity to learn, learn from the best. Who are your role models and mentors? Study the videos or DVDs of those you admire. Keep a notebook or journal in which you write down insights and lessons learned throughout the day. Genuine learning comes from careful observation, not casual looking.

3. Play.

If you think of practicing your craft as play rather than work, you'll find the process much more enjoyable. Play is the application of the principles you've learned. And play casts failure in a whole new light. When we're having fun, we aren't upset by mistakes and errors. We just learn from them and use them to get better.

In the 1950s, Wilson Greatbatch was an assistant professor of engineering at the University of Buffalo, working with cardiologists on a way to record the sound of the human heart. While experimenting with a prototype device one day, he accidentally removed the wrong electrical resistor, a tiny device with wires coming out of each end. Upon checking the electric circuit, he discovered that it pulsed, followed by a one-second delay—very much like a human heartbeat. From that mistake he came up with the heart pacemaker.

Greatbatch observes, "Someone once said that luck favors the prepared mind." The holder of 319 patents, he also says,

"Nine out of ten things I've done have never worked. And that doesn't bother me." Greatbatch worries that society has become far less tolerant of failure: "Failure's a learning experience. The guy who's never failed has never done anything."

A person who has never failed is a person who has never tried. Every remarkable performer I've ever met has failed as often as—and usually more than—he or she has succeeded. And their successes came about only because they were willing to try something new and learn from the experience.

4. Perfect.

The Eagles use their "circle of fear" to perfect new songs. Invariably, the last run-through of a song will be slightly different from the first as they incorporate subtle changes and nuances. It's why so many great novelists, when pressed, refer to themselves as re-writers more than writers. Writing a great novel is not so much a matter of writing and completing it as much as re-writing it until it is polished and ready. Even polished efforts can be perfected just a little bit more.

In the process of executing what we know, we learn new things. The person who believes he knows it all is the person who knows little. Perfection is not a goal but a process—one that never ends.

5. Teach.

My friend Charlie "Tremendous" Jones, whom I mentioned earlier, says, "The greatest way to grow is to teach." Teaching something requires that you really know and understand it; teaching challenges you to go deeper and also raises questions about what you doubt or don't know. If necessity is the mother of invention, repetition is the mother of retention. Do you need to get up to speed on a new product in your company's catalog? Before taking it to customers, volunteer to lead an in-house class explaining the new offering to other sales associates. If you need to prepare for a specialty certification exam in your field, volunteer to lead a study group of other candidates. To increase your parenting or marriage or communication skills, offer to teach a class at your church, in your neighborhood or community, or at a local community college.

The motto of Newark State College is: "Who dares to teach must never cease to learn." I'd paraphrase that sentiment slightly: "Who dares to teach *will* never cease to learn."

Practicing

If you're an athlete or sportsman, it's easy to set up a practice routine: a certain number of free throws, serves, drives, pitches, or hits tuned to meet certain predetermined goals. But what about those of us whose vocation is less quantifiable? How does a police officer, teacher, plumber, pilot, clerk, manager, or parent practice?

Here are five strategies for effective practice that can be applied to any task or environment:

1. Make time to practice.

Few of us *have* time. We're already busy. That means we need to *make* time for the important things each day, and practice is critical if you want to turn in a remarkable performance.

Earlier I mentioned that so many of us "practice in process," or work at getting better as we do our jobs. Is there a way to learn more from practice in process? There is. The way to do that is through noticing *how* you're doing what you're doing and working toward constant improvement.

To get better, you need to know what works and what doesn't. You can learn a lot more by paying attention to what you're doing than by performing on autopilot.

2. *Practice the fundamentals.*

Did you take lessons in piano, clarinet, violin, or some other musical instrument as a kid? If so, you are familiar with practicing the scales. Scales are the fundamentals of music. Practicing them helps make you better and develops your facility in all of the pieces you perform. At work, you can practice your SCALES by using the following:

Summarizing
Critical
Actions
(and)
Learning
Essential
Skills

These are your work performance SCALES.

First, summarize critical actions. These are the components of a remarkable performance. As with a checklist, if you do these things, your success will be assured. Make sure that you examine your performance for those actions that make it remarkable, not just passable.

In sales you could summarize critical actions as qualifying, contacting, presenting, and closing. Those four actions are essential in any successful sale.

What are the related skills? "Qualifying" is based on understanding your product offering and target market. "Contacting" is about scheduling appointments with decision-makers. "Presenting" requires both interpersonal and communication skills. And "closing" is about demonstrating value and persuasion.

If you think in terms of activities and skills, you can break down the elements of any job so that you'll be able to practice to become truly remarkable.

Second, learn essential skills. These are the "pitches, hits, drives, and returns" of workday performance. Knowing what action to take isn't enough—you need to be able to perform the action consistently. Practice is what will take you from conscious effort to consistent mastery.

SCALES can be developed for any performance, at work or at home. With this blueprint for practice, not only will you get better, but you will be on your way to remarkable.

3. Set goals.

To make your performance remarkable, you have to improve. How will you know you've gotten better? By achieving a measurable goal or level of improvement. It doesn't do any good to aim for the next level if you don't know what the next level looks like.

Improvement can be measured any number of ways, but

usually it involves speed, quality, and quantity. Make your goals concrete rather than ambiguous.

VAGUE	MEASURABLE
Sell more	Increase sales by 20 percent
Improve performance	Receive 95+ at next performance review
Spend more time on outbound calls	Devote a minimum of three hours daily to outbound calling
Achieve recognition from management	Qualify for Circle of Excellence by year-end

4. Figure out what works for you.

Some people pursue change by going from hard to easy—tackling the most difficult challenges first. Others like to progress from easy to hard. For example, achieving easy, incremental changes can create momentum to tackle harder goals later. Which method is more effective? That depends on you. Choose the method that works better for you based on your personality and the situation at hand. Be conscious about how you wish to work and make it part of your practice plan.

5. Aim for perfection but don't expect it.

Reframe "imperfection" and "mistakes" as helpful feedback telling you where you need to focus your attention and work harder. The average person becomes frustrated when he or she makes a mistake. Those who become remarkable performers recognize that a mistake is an opportunity to tackle exactly what it is they need to work on and improve. Remarkable performances don't have to be perfect. In fact, they seldom are. Practice may not make perfect, but if done correctly, it will always make you better. It is the one thing that will make all your performances more remarkable.

CHAPTER 8

PERFORMANCE: HOW TO ENGAGE YOUR AUDIENCE

There is nothing worse than a performance that falls flat. Ho-hum performances, whether in the workplace, in the marketplace, or on stage, disappoint. (In the words of a well-known business publication, we either "perform or perish.")

Conversely, there is nothing better than a performance that soars.

At the bagel shop near my home, there is a new manager who always delivers great performance. Recently, he was working the cash register. When an older gentleman in line ahead of me asked for the senior citizen discount, the manager smiled and said, "What? You're trying to fool me, aren't you? You can't be a day over thirty!"—all the while ringing up the man's purchase less the discount. As I approached the register, he said, "Now here's a brother who's hungry! He's eating his bagel before he's even paid for it!" Guilty as charged, I couldn't help smiling as I paid. As I walked away, I heard the manager's banter continue with the next person in line.

You and I have been in situations where such a performance would have fallen flat. It would have been irritating, it would not have been funny, and it would have slowed down the transaction—it would have been a turn-off instead of a turn-on. But that day, in that bagel shop, the manager gave a remarkable performance. He wasn't promoting himself—he was promoting his customers. He wasn't "showing off"—he was warm, engaging, and just humorous enough to add value to what probably would have been a bland transaction in another establishment.

Be the Performance

I never got the impression that the bagel shop manager was acting. Rather, I felt like he was *just being himself*. What he was doing behind the cash register was what he did on his own time with his family and friends: making people feel good about his role in their lives.

One hallmark of a remarkable performance is authenticity. There is harmony between the performance and the performer.

My point is this: build your reputation and your brand on authenticity, not hyperbole.

The truth is that there are no innately boring jobs in this world, no boring careers or vocations, and no boring interchanges between people. When we have what we consider a boring or uninspiring experience or exchange, it's almost always because the other person involved is unengaged or unimaginative. Turning bland into grand is part of what makes a performance remarkable.

Regardless of how much practice and preparation you have done, the success of your performance lies in your ability to engage your audience.

If you engage your audience, if you capture and hold them from the beginning, why would they not call you back for an encore? Who likes to see something thoroughly enjoyable come to an end?

Think about your favorite movie or CD, the best concert you ever attended, the most romantic evening or exciting weekend you ever spent. I'll bet those are experiences that you wished would never end. You may have gone back to the same resort or city or re-rented the movie, just to try to re-create that same feeling.

And that's how you want your employer, customer, colleague, or spouse to respond to you—by calling you back for more.

To create the Encore Effect, you shouldn't be focused on your own happiness or success, but on the happiness and success of others. We all tend to repeat the experiences in life that have a positive impact on us. And when you have a positive impact on others, they'll want to repeat the experience in the same way.

Connecting with Your Audience

So how do you connect with your audience?

1. Invite attention.

The biggest obstacle when you begin a performance is your audience's preoccupation.

People in sales are taught that they have thirty to sixty seconds to make the sale. I'm not sure that is literally true, but I agree in principle: if you don't capture or engage the client or customer right away, you'll probably never get the order.

The same is true whatever your vocation. Everyone you meet has a full plate. Their lives are filled with agendas, desires, distractions, concerns, and the clutter of everyday life. Your job is to break through that debris and capture their attention.

Every time you perform you are competing against the rest of the world for the attention of your audience.

- The customer coming into the big-box hardware retail store looking for a power drill is also thinking about his tight budget, his two kids who are hungry and getting antsy, the other errands on his to-do list, and his concerns about the rumored job cuts at his office. The salesman's job is to engage with the customer in a way that trumps those competing priorities and helps the customer obtain what he came into the store to get.

- The mother with a small child who is listening to a nurse explain a medical procedure has competing concerns as well. She is worried that she'll make a mistake and harm her child; she wonders whether her insurance will cover the cost; she's concerned about picking up her other child from day care on time. The nurse's job is to break through the preoccupied mother's concerns long enough to convey the information the mother needs to know.

You and I know what it feels like to be preoccupied. As performers, we need to recognize the other demands on our customers or colleagues and do whatever it takes to reach through that sixty-second window and capture their attention. And remember this: *The best way to capture another person's attention is to give them all of yours.*

2. Ignite their interest.

Imagine it's cold, the wind is blowing, and people are scurrying to work or their next appointment. But in the midst of the morning hustle and bustle a small crowd forms on the sidewalk—and it's slowly getting larger.

Someone has ignited the interest of passersby—people who had no intention of interrupting their day to watch someone perform on a sidewalk. Whether the crowd is forming to hear music, observe an argument, watch street acrobatics, or see a product being demonstrated, the performer has captured the attention of his or her audience.

And that is one of the secrets of remarkable performance—igniting your audience's interest.

A friend of mine who is a judge told me about a med student intern he encountered who wore a white doctor's lab coat that was custom-tailored. He wanted a way to stand out among the other interns as they made rounds and met doctors and patients. The result of his tailored clothes? There was "something about" the intern: no one could identify it, but in a group he was the one who stood out—the one who ignited interest.

Igniting interest is a critical step toward getting a yes to the question "Will you marry me?" or "Will you hire me?" People who are uninteresting do not get the nod, whether in romance, business, or life. And again: *The best way to get others interested in you is to be interested in them.*

3. Involve the audience.

The single best way to engage any audience in any circumstance is to get them involved—intellectually, emotionally, and/or physically. When you do so, they become part of the performance.

Intellectual involvement gets people thinking. Look for opportunities to ask them questions like:

- What do you think about this?

- What questions come to mind?

- How will you use this information?

Emotional involvement gets people to feel. Great performers in any venue appeal to both the head and the heart. One way to get people to connect emotionally to what you're doing is by weaving a story into what you present. Ask: "How do you feel about that?"

I can hear some reader saying, "Hey, I'm an accountant! My colleagues want accurate numbers and information. What's that got to do with feelings?" The answer: everything. Accurate numbers and data can—and should—elicit emotions, whether those emotions are fear, security, confidence, or elation. Be aware of the emotions you create.

Finally, even better than watching is doing. Get your audience involved in a hands-on way. What is it about your performance that would allow audience members to participate? Could they "try out" or demonstrate what you've just explained?

These tips will help you connect with your audience intellectually, emotionally, and physically:

- *Be attractive*. Attractiveness isn't about genetics—it's about demeanor, appearance, and appeal. To do good, look good. To get into a person's or group's consciousness, you have only five senses available. Use them all.

- *Tell stories*. Make your stories brief, interesting, and illustrative; humor helps.

- *Show more than tell*. An object or picture invites another person to share your space, which then becomes "our" space.

- *Don't try to manufacture passion*. If you don't have it before you begin, trying to fake passion will hurt more than help your cause.

- *Move around*. Movement creates interest. It's harder for people's attention to wander when their eyes are following you.

- *Exceed expectations*. Think of what your audience is expecting and then surprise them by doing more. Always provide a surprise.

- *Really* look *at people*. Watch people doing interviews on television or communicating in real life—too many of them rarely look at the person to whom they're speaking!

- *Ask questions, especially at the outset*. A question invites another person to demonstrate his knowledge or give her opinion; questions convey the sense that you value what the other person thinks or believes.

- *Use humor gracefully and graciously.*

- *Listen as much as, if not more than, you talk.*

- *Stay engaged after you leave*. Thank-you notes, calls, and small gifts (if appropriate) will keep interest alive.

Remember: *If you want your audience to be involved with you, you have to get involved with them and what they think, feel, and do.*

4. Include extras.

A recent *U.S. News & World Report* article on top leaders in the United States spent as much time highlighting how much these leaders did *outside* their immediate organizations. They mentored others, supported worthy and charitable causes, brought people together, and challenged the status quo. In other words, they used these "extras" to make themselves, and their companies, even more attractive.

What "extras" do you bring to your performance? When someone takes your hand, how many other hands are they grasping?

Remember: *The extras you offer give your audience—your customers, colleagues, friends, or direct reports—yet another reason to choose you out of a crowded field of performers.*

5. Inspire action.

When you've finished giving a performance, the answer that will determine whether or not you've given a remarkable performance is this: So what? What have you accomplished? What have you inspired your audience to do?

Stephen Covey, the famous author of *The Seven Habits of Highly Effective People*, among other books, has long counseled his audiences to "begin with the end in mind." If you don't know what you want your audience to come away with at the end of your performance (whether a single performance or a year's worth of performances), then you have no idea how to perform.

Here's a list of some specific "ends." Do you know what you need to do to achieve them?

- An offer of a job

- An offer of a raise, promotion, new benefit, or increased responsibility

- Acceptance of a proposal (marriage, business partnership, new project)

- Acceptance of discipline or correction

- A sale

- Achievement of a goal

- An offer of a favor, contribution, loan, or commitment of support

Every activity or effort we undertake in life results in an end. We rarely get up in the morning and say, "I could care less what happens today." Unfortunately, however, we too often live as if we feel that way—out of fear, discomfort, boredom, or fatigue.

Remember: *Know what actions you want your audience to take. It will inform everything you do.*

When your audience requests an encore, it is not asking for a repeat *performance* as much as for more face time with the *performer*. When you engage your audience, you become the performance, and your performances become how you are known.

CHAPTER 9

POLISH:
MAKING YOUR
PERFORMANCE SHINE

Thom Winninger is a successful entrepreneur, author, and speaker. As a kid, he spent summers living with his grandfather. Growing up, Thom had a bit of a speech impediment and called his grandpa 'Ampa.

In his spare time, 'Ampa built and refinished furniture that he sold as collectibles, and he was teaching Thom to do the same. It was Thom's job to finish the pieces that 'Ampa built.

One day a woman arrived at the workshop in tears holding pieces of a piano bench that held great sentimental value for her. "Can you fix this?" she asked, fearing the answer would be no. Her fears were justified—unfortunately, the piece was too damaged to repair. So Thom's grandfather offered to build an identical piece from scratch. He led her to the back of the shop where he kept different types of wood and guided her in the selection process. He told the woman he'd have the piano bench finished in four weeks.

Sadly, 'Ampa died of a stroke before she came back to pick up the piece.

But 'Ampa had already completed the building of the piano bench and had given Thom instructions for finishing the job. All that remained was applying the finish.

Thom and his grandfather had been using an Old World concoction of linseed oil applied by hand. The oils from their hands combined with the linseed to penetrate the wood deeper and deeper.

'Ampa believed that people were attracted to the furniture he created not because of the value of the pieces themselves, although they were of the highest quality, but because the finish allowed the buyer to see himself or herself in the reflection of the piece, creating a deep sense of ownership. People responded to seeing something of themselves in the work.

Just before his grandfather passed away, he gave Thom his final instructions, not only for the piano bench but, as Thom now believes, for the rest of his life:

"You just keep polishing that bench until the woman comes to pick it up. The finish, you see, is never done."

The reason I relate this story is that I believe 'Ampa's instruction applies equally to the secret of being a remarkable performer. Each of us must keep polishing until "the woman comes to pick it up." And that means never taking details for granted. The polishing is what makes any performance truly shine and reflects the commitment of the performer.

The Difference Is in the Details

Nineteenth-century French novelist Gustave Flaubert is credited with the observation that "God is in the details." German
pop musician Blixa Bargeld is credited with the opposite view:
"The devil is in the details."

It turns out that both were right as far as remarkable performances are concerned. More often than not when we perform
remarkably, our success can be attributed to our attention to the
details. And if we perform poorly, it was a lack of attention to
detail that probably did us in.

Richard Carlson wrote a national best-seller entitled *Don't
Sweat the Small Stuff.* I agree with the thesis of his book—that too
many people spend their lives worrying about things that they
either can't control or that won't make any real difference in
their lives. There's no sense contributing to one's risk of hyper-
tension and cardiac arrest worrying about things that don't
matter.

The danger of "not sweating the small stuff" as a philosophy,
however, is that it provides a "Get Out of Details-Jail Free" card
to people who justify not doing their best. By not sweating any of
the small stuff, they're not bothering to separate the details that
don't matter from those that do.

And trust me: there are *lots* of details that matter when it
comes to creating a remarkable performance.

Here are some excuses people tell themselves to avoid rolling
up their sleeves and dealing with the nitty-gritty of achieving a
remarkable performance.

- "I know I should format and print up a proposal before I
  make my sales call. But I'm out of time—it's Friday, and

this guy wants to leave for the weekend. At the end of the day, he's either going to buy or not."

· "I told my daughter we were going to do something special for her sixteenth birthday. But I got busy with work and failed to follow through. Hey, my job pays for these gifts! I know she'll understand, eventually. And I'll make it up to her."

· "I got passed over for the promotion—again! I'm done trying. What is the point of talking to my boss about how I might improve? He's already made up his mind about me. I am who I am, and if that's not good enough for him, then so be it."

Have you ever thought this way?

My point is this: our failure to take that extra step—to polish our performance by paying close attention to the fine details—can make all the difference. It can separate you and your performance from everyone else's, and it can transform a performance that is good into one that is remarkable.

Think about what an extra step might mean to those we just heard from:

· The client at the sales call might think to himself: "This is the sharpest young sales guy I've ever met—and on a Friday afternoon no less. If he treats our company with the same care and respect he applied to his proposal, we'll be in good hands. I'm going to give him a shot."

· The sixteen-year-old daughter might not say: "Dad, I can't believe you took the red-eye back from California just so we could go out to dinner for my birthday." But she'll remember that her father was there for her. And what might have been a missed opportunity could turn out to be the one birthday she'll never forget.

· The boss might say: "Billy, I know it's not easy to miss out on a promotion you wanted. But I'm impressed that you came to talk to me about it. Yes, I can tell you the specific reasons I chose someone else. If you're willing to work on a couple of areas, I can assure you that your future is secure with our company."

The British philosopher Alfred North Whitehead once observed, "We think in generalities, but we live in the detail." Whitehead was one of the greatest mathematicians who ever lived. Think about the details in a mathematical formula filling a blackboard. The answer will come out wrong if even a single step—a plus sign written as a minus sign in step 3_1—is wrong. That same level of detail is important in the calculus of our lives and careers as well. Frederick Faber noted, "Exactness in little things is a wonderful source of cheerfulness." His unusual choice of the word "cheerfulness" has important implications.

I would argue that we feel most satisfied and secure—most cheerful, to use Faber's word—when we know that we have done everything we could to ensure a remarkable performance.

And we feel our worst when we know we could have (and should have) done better.

There are two times to polish your performance and tend to the details that can make a difference: pre-performance and post-performance. Remarkable performers take care of both.

When a team of entrepreneurs is trying to sell their new company to stock analysts on the eve of an IPO, they practice their "dog-and-pony show" relentlessly. Then, when the presentation is over, they do a postmortem: What went right? What went wrong? What questions did we not have answers for? What do we need to tweak? They polish before *and* after every presentation.

Why? Because there are tens, maybe hundreds, of millions of dollars on the line. Even more important is their self-esteem, their desire to be successful, their desire to tell the world that their business is remarkable.

Is your own performance any less important?

Pre-Performance: Polishing Your Performance Before You Take the Stage

Regardless of how many times you've been through the routine—the same sales call, the same committee meeting, the same date with your spouse, the same hospital rounds—each time is different! To say, "I don't need to prepare," demeans the event and overvalues your skills. Every event in life is worth the time it takes to polish the details. Top athletes practice relentlessly before an event. Musicians, actors, and other performers of all sorts do the same.

Here are three things you can do to polish your performance in advance:

1. Practice the discipline of "two levels up."

Most of us talk or think about achieving the "next level" in our lives or careers. But if everybody is striving for the next level, then soon enough the next level will become simply today's present level. That means *you* are going to have to strive to reach *two* levels up.

Write "2LU" (two levels up) on drafts of your plans and proposals to remind yourself to aim higher. Use sticky notes and put them where you'll see them: on your laptop, your desk, your bathroom mirror, your bathroom scales—wherever you want to think about what you are doing *before* you do it.

2. Take a lesson from a baker.

In thirteenth-century England, bakers could lose a hand (or worse) for selling a dozen rolls or buns but being one short. This is the origin of the expression "baker's dozen," meaning thirteen. Bakers decided it was safer to add an additional roll to an order for a dozen to make sure that they never fell short—and that they could keep their hands to bake another day.

What is the equivalent of a "baker's dozen" in your world? What will ensure that you don't get caught short? Extra preparation, extra polish, extra attention to detail—however that translates in your world—can determine whether you receive a second order (an encore) or not.

3. Don't settle for excellence.

Since Tom Peters and Robert Waterman's 1982 mega-bestseller *In Search of Excellence*, "excellence" has arguably become the most widely used performance term in our culture.

But excellence suggests a quantifiable standard that can be copied. I would argue that instead of settling for excellence, we should strive for distinction. What do I mean by that? Distinctiveness, by definition, refers to "one and only one." When you are distinctive, you possess something no one else has. You are second to none in your area of excellence. Distinctiveness almost demands an encore performance.

Guitar legend Les Paul, still performing today in his nineties, tells a story about his mother calling him in the early days of his career. She told him she had heard him on the radio. Les knew that the person she heard hadn't been him, but someone who sounded like him. That was the moment he decided to become distinctive: "I don't want the same sounds. I want sounds that have never been heard before."

What can make your performance distinctive?

Post-Polish: Polish Your Performance
After the Curtain Comes Down

The tendency after a performance is to breathe a sigh of relief and head for home. Stop. Think of debriefing as an integral part of your performance. Don't kick off your shoes until you've identified what needs polishing before you take the stage again. Here's how:

1. Focus on the power of a mistake.

Pain is the natural result of a fall, whether from a stepladder in your home or from an embarrassing failure in a performance. That pain, whether physical or emotional, is capable of demanding all your attention.

Don't focus on the pain you felt when you landed. Instead, focus on the step you took just before you fell. What caused you to fall? Your misstep might have been unpreventable—accidents happen. But lack of preparation is a more likely cause of failure. Identify why the misstep occurred and what you need to fix to prevent it from happening again.

2. Solicit others' ideas for improvement.

Ask for feedback about your performance, but remember: opinions are free, and many of them are worth what you pay for them. Learn to distinguish between those individuals who give helpful feedback and those whose critique shouldn't carry much weight. The people whose feedback I value most give it to me pointedly, honestly, and briefly. They tell me things I can do to make *my* performance better, not how *they* would have done it differently. They focus on what I did and what I can do to improve.

Thus, when you're soliciting feedback after a performance from those people whose opinions you care about, don't begin by saying, "If you had been in my place. . . ." Instead, say to them, "You know me and what I was trying to accomplish today," before asking:

- What was the most effective part of my performance?

- What was the least effective part?

- If I gave the same performance again in one hour, how could I make it better?

- If someone else asks you how I did today, what will you tell him or her?

3. Explain, don't complain.

Complaining is the act of shirking responsibility for things that go wrong. Explaining is the act of demonstrating that you understand what went wrong. If a less-than-stellar performance or result wasn't your fault, don't complain about it. Instead, determine what steps you can take next time that will improve it and that are in your control.

The best revenge in response to a subpar performance is to approach the future with a solution in hand.

Your next performance will be the same as your previous performance—plus whatever details you have chosen to polish. Like the makers of fine furniture, remarkable performers are those who never stop polishing.

CHAPTER 10

PITFALLS:
HOW TO KEEP
FROM STUMBLING

When Jessica Clements joined the Army Reserve at age eighteen as a high school senior, she planned on putting in twenty uneventful years and retiring at age thirty-eight, ready for a second career. Nine years later, on May 5, 2004, a roadside bomb in Iraq put a big crimp in that plan.

Her injuries were life-threatening. Doctors in Germany stabilized her before she was flown to Walter Reed Army Hospital in the United States. Three weeks after her injury, she woke up from the coma she'd been in. After three and a half years spent relearning how to walk, talk, read, and write, as well as getting her half-skull reattached, she was back to her beautiful, upbeat self.

As she told another wounded soldier at Walter Reed, "Stay positive, okay? You get strong. No matter how bad it hurts, you keep going. That's how you have to do it. We're soldiers. That's what we do best."

Jessica reminds me of words often heard but not always followed: it isn't what happens to us that matters most, but what we do about it.

Life is full of pitfalls. While they vary in seriousness, a single fall can undo a remarkable performance. In this chapter, I want to talk about how to deal with those pitfalls, both those we create and those we can't control.

Not If, but When

Encountering pitfalls in life is not a matter of *if*, but *when*:

- You have a presentation ready for an important client. Everyone is gathered in the conference room. Just as you are about to begin, the power goes out—as does your carefully crafted PowerPoint presentation.

- You and your spouse are having a romantic anniversary dinner—in Paris, atop the Eiffel Tower. You ask the waiter at the fancy restaurant to take a picture, but when you turn the camera on, it's dead. You forgot to recharge the battery.

- You have an interview with the president of a Wall Street firm to discuss your consulting company's services. You have a half-hour window for the interview. But traffic is a nightmare, and you realize that you'll never make your appointment on time.

Pitfalls happen. Sometimes they are preventable, and sometimes they are not. The key is to prevent the pitfalls and problems you can and to be prepared to deal with the ones you cannot.

Preventable Pitfalls

1. Arrogance

St. Benedict said, "Nothing can damage me but myself." He was referring to self-inflicted performance pitfalls. When we have a higher estimation of ourselves, or a lower estimation of others, than we should, we are setting ourselves up for a fall. Nothing will cause others to withdraw their support faster than an air of superiority on our part. While most people respect the confidence of someone who turns in a remarkable performance, no one appreciates arrogance. The antidote to arrogance is humility.

Pastor Rick Warren says that humility isn't thinking less of yourself, but thinking of yourself less.

2. Complacency

Complacency comes about when we feel that "acceptable" is good enough.

When we're complacent, we tend to coast or get by on past performance. Even when our past performance was remarkable, it doesn't guarantee that our present-day or future performances will be remarkable. Standards are often raised, the performances of others improve, and what was once our "best" can easily turn into "good" or, worse, "average."

The antidote to complacency is commitment. Commitment is a willingness to continually learn and improve. It is about investing a little more in the pursuit of getting better, regardless of how good you are now.

3. Lethargy or Procrastination

Lazy people often have great intentions—they just never seem to accomplish any of them. "Never accomplish today what can be put off until tomorrow."

What is the antidote to lethargy? Energy. The ability to get work done. Energy infuses a good performance with the something extra that can make it great. Remarkable performers don't sleepwalk through their work. Their stores of energy come from the knowledge that what they are doing matters.

4. Fear

Fear, which is caused by threats both real and imagined, can be immobilizing. When it comes to performance, nothing creates more fear than a lack of preparation. The antidote to fear is confidence, and confidence results from preparation and practice. Knowing *how* to do something and repeated success at doing it instill confidence. Fear is based on the unknown; confidence is based on the certain knowledge of yourself and your abilities.

5. Apathy

Apathetic people are telling others, "I don't care." The antidote to apathy is concern. Concern says, "I care." It comes from the fundamental belief that what you're doing and those for whom you're doing it are important. Apathy may be the most devastating pitfall of all because it denies the natural drive of the human spirit to move onward and upward. Concern for your work, for your customers and colleagues, for your patient or congregation, is critical to remarkable performance. It is an emotion that moves us from self-absorption to genuine service to others.

6. Impatience

For every "overnight" success there are dozens of overnight disasters. Too many of us are impatient to reach our goals. We underestimate how long it will take to learn and perfect our craft. We demand success and achievement today—and respond inappropriately when it doesn't happen. People who are impatient tend to blame others, run over those who stand in the way, and give up when things don't happen as expected (or demanded).

The antidote to impatience is patience—or better, persistence. Persistence is an ongoing effort in the face of challenge. We learn a little and apply it; when we've mastered that much, we learn a little bit more and apply that. More often than not, we achieve the goal of a remarkable performance, not by dashing at it, but by inching ourselves forward.

How to Use the Pointed Stick

We all fall prey at times to the self-inflicted pitfalls just described. But once we are aware of our weak spots and foibles, we can be on guard against them, we can actively engage them, and we can apply the antidotes to the problems.

Robert Fripp, founder of the band King Crimson, is regarded as one of the half-dozen greatest guitarists in the history of rock music. As a mentor and teacher to young guitar students in his League of Crafty Guitarists, Fripp regularly exposes them to what he calls the "pointed stick."

Within a couple days of composing a new piece, Fripp's students are required to perform it in a public venue where there are certain to be "pointed sticks"—crying babies, poor acoustics, inferior audio equipment, hecklers in the audience, and other distractions. By finding ways to surmount the difficulties of performing in a place where things are certain to go wrong, students build their confidence.

When Aristotle was training his student Demosthenes in oratory, he made Demosthenes practice speaking with a mouth full of pebbles. When Tiger Woods started playing golf, his father would deliberately cough or make other distracting noises as Tiger began his swing. Woods has become one of the greatest golfers of all time, especially when playing under pressure.

Similarly, sometimes accepting the most challenging assignments in your field can be a way to strengthen your performance. Performing under less than ideal circumstances can help you to improve your skill, build endurance, and develop a thick skin.

Arrange for a few "pointed sticks" in your day. It may be just the thing to help build your confidence and create a more remarkable performance.

Remember: life is not fair, and remarkable performers know it. There are a great many variables in life that are beyond our control. We need to find ways to achieve a memorable performance in spite of them.

Think of the remarkable performers in history who could have used their circumstances in life as an excuse not to excel. Perhaps they were born with a certain color of skin, or lacked formal education, or had religious beliefs that others looked down on. Perhaps their family lacked financial advantages, or they were the victim of an injustice.

People such as Martin Luther King Jr., Mohandas Gandhi, Harriet Tubman, Abraham Lincoln, and Mother Teresa would never have made an impact on the world had they allowed their disadvantages to hold them back.

Think about your own performance at work. The raw material of the lives of these famous individuals is the same raw material you work with every day. At the beginning, these men and women didn't consciously move toward greatness. They were simply choosing to perform as well as they possibly could, every day.

To paraphrase General George S. Patton, the great things a person does appear to be great only in hindsight. What history ultimately calls great is what an individual with a choice to make decided was right and good as he or she stood at a crossroads in life.

Unfair and unfortunate circumstances surround remarkable performers every day. But instead of being bitter and succumbing to circumstances, they row steadily against the tide until they catch the wind of fortune.

Expect the Unexpected

Remarkable performers do two things in life consistently:

1. They prepare as conscientiously and thoroughly as they can.

2. They remain on the lookout for those random events and circumstances, as well as self-inflicted problems, that could ruin their performance.

Every performer, over a career or a lifetime, has some subpar performances. If the disappointing performance is due to a preventable pitfall, remarkable performers take responsibility immediately, looking for ways to correct the problem. When it is due to something outside their control, they use the experience as an opportunity to grow.

But they don't allow themselves to be paralyzed with guilt or regret or blame.

Chef Grant Achatz opened his restaurant Alinea in Chicago in 2005. The prestigious Mobil guide named it the best restaurant in America. Not bad for a thirty-one-year-old chef. Two years later, he was diagnosed with a cancerous tumor in his tongue. Treatment had the potential for leaving him without the ability to taste. How could a chef who can't taste his creations continue to cook—and to perform remarkably?

"I never said 'I'm done' or 'What am I going to do?' or 'Do I have to change careers?'" Achatz said. The owner of the restaurant said, "You could take out his tongue and his eyes, and it would [still] be Grant's restaurant. I can't imagine that he wouldn't be able to overcome any limitations."

Chef Achatz is a role model for the attitude you have to have, and the actions you have to take, to be a remarkable performer whatever the circumstances.

PART THREE

Sharing
the
Encore Effect

CHAPTER 11

HOW TO HELP OTHERS
PERFORM REMARKABLY

My life was changed one weekend in Dayton, Ohio, by a man I'd never met before. It happened when I was a sophomore at The Ohio State University in Columbus. I heard about an air show scheduled in Dayton, seventy-five miles away. It sounded fun, so I decided to check it out.

I was not disappointed.

Lots of amazing pilots flew that day, but one in particular grabbed my attention: Bob Hoover. Though I didn't know it at the time, I was watching a legend. After his adventures during World War II, Hoover returned to the United States to serve as a military test pilot. After injuries from a test-flight crash limited his high-performance flying, he became the right-hand man of the famed test pilot Chuck Yeager during the latter's rise to stardom.

After leaving the military in 1948, Hoover served as a flight consultant to manufacturers and the military, testing and demonstrating the capabilities of new planes as they came on line. This expertise led to his becoming the greatest aerobatic flier of his day. He was given every award and distinction imaginable, and the Smithsonian's National Air and Space Museum named him the third-greatest aviator in history.

At the time I first saw him that day in Dayton, Ohio, I didn't know who Bob Hoover was. He flew a twin-engine business plane, performing rolls, loops, stalls, and dives—maneuvers not normally associated with business planes. It was a truly remarkable performance.

His final maneuver made my jaw drop. After shutting down both engines in midair, he did a loop followed by an eight-point hesitation slow roll: instead of just rolling the plane, he rolled it slowly and methodically in eight discrete segments, a level of precision that requires incredible skill. Then he gradually glided back to earth and the runway—*still without power!* He touched down, first on one tire, then on the other, then on both, and coasted silently all the way back to the announcer's stand, where he stopped, acknowledging the wildly cheering crowd.

Remarkable!

That was the day I decided I wanted to fly. And before I graduated from college, I had my pilot's license.

I met Bob Hoover a number of years later at the Reno Air Races and thanked him for his role in forming my love of aviation. But I also thanked him for being an example of how a remarkable performance can inspire others.

Inspiring Others

Somewhere in our lives or careers, all of us have been inspired by someone.

Perhaps you were inspired by a third-grade teacher who introduced you to science or writing, or by an attorney who, later in your life, fought for your rights and won.

Yet few remarkable performers see themselves as "inspirational." More often than not, they are simply doing the best they can.

Abraham Lincoln said, "God must love common people 'cause He made so many of 'em." The fact is that we're all common people. Not many of us expect to be famous; moreover, the influence of the famous is limited. But common people performing in uncommon ways are remarkable because they remind us that we are all capable of so much more in our work and lives.

Ask yourself:

· Who has inspired you?

· Who are you inspiring? Think about those around you, how they view you, what their needs are, how they've been affected by knowing you.

Bob Hoover didn't know that a wide-eyed, impressionable college kid was in the crowd that day. He just did what he did every time he got into the cockpit of a plane: performing to the best of his ability, he performed remarkably.

How many other people in the crowd at the Dayton Air Show

and at other air shows like it were inspired to take up flying as a result of Hoover's performance? I'm sure I'm not alone.

Everywhere we go the effects of our performance are having an impact on the people around us—some whom we know and others who may remain unknown to us.

Reach Those Whom You Teach

Dr. Bruce Wilkinson has written several best-selling books, including *The Prayer of Jabez* (number one on the *New York Times* best-seller list) and *The Dream Giver*. In a lesser-known book he wrote for teachers—*The Seven Laws of the Learner*—he makes this point: it is the teacher's responsibility to cause the student to learn.

Wilkinson recounts that he was called into the academic dean's office at the college where he was teaching to explain why all his students had received an A in his course. The dean's assumption was that Wilkinson had made the course too easy, since the grades didn't follow the normal distribution curve. After examining the course syllabus and final exam, the dean realized that the course in fact was closer to the graduate than the undergraduate level, and he wondered how Wilkinson had done it.

In essence, Wilkinson decided what a well-educated student in the subject should know and then had his students learn that same material. Then he tested them to prove to him and to themselves that they had indeed learned the material. So he gave them all an A.

Wilkinson taught remarkably, and his students learned remarkably.

He didn't *teach* by just presenting the material; he was able to *reach* students and cause them to learn.

How many people in our lives do we intentionally reach? How many would say that they are better because of how we affected them? And how many are we consciously *trying* to reach?

Too many people miss the opportunity to raise their game to a higher level by not taking advantage of opportunities to teach and reach others—whether as an instructor, a mentor, a boss, a peer, or a parent.

"But what do I know that is so important?" you might ask. "Who needs me to teach others anything?" Whatever your age, your skill level, your expertise, or your knowledge, someone in your world could benefit from what you've learned. Those are the people you can choose to reach.

Obviously, parents teach their children and educators teach their students. But friends should offer to teach each other. And bosses and managers should teach those under them, just as pastors and religious leaders need to teach their flocks. Craftspeople must teach their apprentices. The list goes on and on.

If you're already doing this, let me encourage you to not just teach, but *reach*!

In teaching, you might tell a colleague:

> *Okay, Jill, create a new document by clicking here,*
> *then do your work, then save it by hitting Alt-S on the*
> *keyboard. And you're done. Okay? Call me if you need*
> *anything.*

When you *reach*, you might tell a colleague:

Jill, I've really been impressed with how quickly you've learned your way around our office routines. You seem to pick up things quickly. I'm sure this software will be a breeze for someone like you. I don't claim to be an expert at it, but I'm going to make sure you know how to use the functions we depend on here in the office. Okay, let's start at the beginning. [A thorough demonstration takes place, including time spent with the Help features and the manual.] *I'm available to help. If you get stuck, just let me know. My goal is to see you become productive and confident as quickly as possible.*

Which of these two teachers would have reached you? If you were Jill, which teacher would have gotten the better response from you? I think the answer is clear. Teachers who reach others communicate not just ideas and information but compassion and commitment.

Here are some simple ways to transform teaching into *reaching*:

- Get the individual's commitment to the idea that raising his or her performance level is a worthwhile endeavor.

- Communicate the "why" as well as the "what" and the "how." It is the why—the reasons we have for wanting to achieve remarkable performance—that speaks to our inner motivation and desire to do better.

- Explain the benefits. Paint a picture of what the future might look like so that the individual can see how his or her life will be better by learning what you are teaching.

- Invest yourself. Become a partner-in-progress with the person you are trying to reach. Knowing you'll be there to ensure his or her success will convey commitment and concern.

- Assume responsibility for helping the individual's progress and performance. Assist that person in being remarkable. And don't quit until that goal is achieved.

Improve by Encouraging

Encouragement is the grease that allows the wheels of *inspiration* and *instruction* to turn efficiently. Think about how you respond to encouragement. Those around you need it in the same way.

Henry Drummond, author of the timeless best-seller *The Greatest Thing in the World*, wrote, "You will find, if you think for a moment, that the people who influence you are people who believe in you."

Who do you know (besides your family) who believes in you? Having such people in your life can move you from routine to remarkable in all sorts of ways.

In whom do you believe? How many people have been the recipients of your encouragement? To have friends you have to be a friend. Similarly, to be encouraged you have to encourage others.

The best way I know to encourage others is by giving them feedback. By feedback I do not mean unsolicited advice, criticism, or an account of how you would have done it yourself. Only after you've established a relationship with another person and earned the right to speak about their life will that person know that you have only their best interests in mind. Until then, feedback will come across as criticism or unwelcome advice. And it will be counterproductive.

When you are encouraging others, you might say, "I think so highly of you that I want you to reach a level of performance that is higher than you believe you can achieve. I believe you can reach it. And I want to encourage you to believe it as well."

Remarkable performers see in others what they have discovered in themselves—the ability to reach unexplored and unanticipated levels of performance. They *inspire* others through their own performances, *instruct* others through their teaching, and help others *improve* through their encouragement.

CHAPTER 12

FROM REMARKABLE PERFORMER TO REMARKABLE PERSON

By any measure, James Barksdale has been a remarkable performer in the world of business.

He is best known as the CEO of Netscape Communications Corporation from 1995 to 1999, the company that opened up the Internet to the world via its Netscape Web browser. Before Netscape, Barksdale had been the CEO of McCaw Cellular/AT&T Wireless, and before that the vice president and COO of FedEx.

As impressive as his business success has been, that's not what Jim Barksdale is best known for. His encore has been more about giving money away than making it.

Even before leaving Netscape, Barksdale and his late wife gave generously to their state's education system, the University of Mississippi, and a scholarship fund for the University of Mississippi Medical Center.

But it was the Barksdales' gift of $100 million in 2000 that focused attention on Barksdale the person instead of Barksdale the performer. Distributed among seven Mississippi universities to equip teachers with better skills for teaching children to read, this gift remains the largest private donation for a child education initiative in U.S. history.

The English writer John Ruskin said, "The highest reward for a person's toil is not what he gets for it, but what he becomes by it." In Barksdale's case, it was also about what he helped others become through his generosity.

When AOL bought Netscape in 1999, Jim Barksdale departed with $700 million. That's what he received for his toil. But what he *became* by his toil was a person determined to be of larger service to others.

The ultimate benefit—indeed, the ultimate purpose—of a remarkable performance is to become a remarkable person—and vice versa.

Remarkable performances often result in increased rewards. These rewards may include money, but they also come as increased exposure, recognition, influence, and opportunity.

The question is, how will you use the rewards of your own remarkable performances? Will you use them to promote and satisfy only yourself? That is your prerogative, but there is a greater opportunity: to serve and have a positive impact on those around you.

It has been said that increased opportunity and means in life don't make us different as much as they *reveal* who we really are. Distinguishing between remarkable *performances* and remarkable *people* is like asking which came first—the chicken or the egg?

The person who strives to perform more remarkably without also focusing on becoming a more remarkable person is missing the larger point.

How do we promote growth in both areas at the same time?

I believe that there are six areas of focus that, when developed and mastered, can't help but make anyone a remarkable person.

I picture them in terms of an inverted pyramid, with *potential* as the foundation for being remarkable and *personalization* as the highest expression of it:

THE PYRAMID OF POSSIBILITY

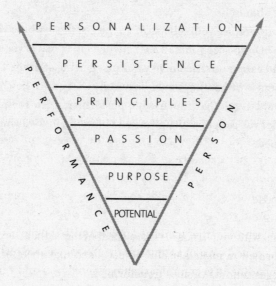

The Pyramid of Possibility

Potential

Our potential—both individually and collectively—has no known limits. Many of us know how good we are at our jobs and responsibilities, but none of us knows how good we *could* be. That is the magic and mystery of our potential.

Do you ever think: "I've advanced as far as I can go. I've maxed out my potential."

Johann Wolfgang von Goethe, the famous nineteenth-century German poet and novelist, wrote, "Treat a man as he appears to be, and you make him worse. But treat a man as if he already were what he potentially could be, and you make him what he should be."

How do you see yourself? How do you see those whom you influence? Do you see yourself as "finished" in terms of your spiritual and career advancement or as just getting started? Do you see others for what they could be or only as they are now?

I would argue that remarkable performers view themselves and others as people with unlimited potential, just waiting to be developed.

Purpose

Potential without purpose is like a sheet of metal that has not yet been formed to make a useful object. Feed that sheet of metal into a press and its value is transformed.

Every human being has unlimited potential. But we need the press of purpose to create a channel for expression and action. Purpose focuses potential.

Viktor Frankl was a Jewish psychiatrist who was arrested by the Nazis during World War II. He hid the manuscript of a book on which he had labored for years—a book on the importance of finding meaning and purpose in life—in the lining of his coat. But the Nazis took his coat, and his manuscript was lost. Stripped of every material possession, he began to wonder if his life had any meaning as he waited to die in a concentration camp.

In the pocket of a ragged garment he was given to wear in the camps, he found a tiny scrap of paper on which a prisoner had written a Hebrew scripture from the Old Testament. He took that discovery not as a coincidence but as a message: he needed to live out his convictions concerning meaning in life and not just write about them in a book.

He survived the camps. As he later wrote in his book *Man's Search for Meaning*, "There is nothing in the world that would so effectively help one to survive even the worst conditions, as the knowledge that there is a meaning in one's life." Frankl believed that searching for and finding that meaning was critical not just to survival but to a spiritually fulfilling life as well.

Remarkable performers have not only recognized their potential but discovered the purpose—the mold, the channel, the press—that will give shape and add value to their potential.

Passion

Passion is the fire-in-the-belly that we bring to human endeavors. Of course, passion that is not tied to purpose is like lightning firing in the sky: who knows where it will land and what kind of damage it will do? But electricity that has a purpose—well, that's a different story. That kind of energy can run a household or light up a city.

As the philosopher Thomas Hobbes put it, "Passions unguided are of the most part mere madness."

Passion is the emotional energy you bring to your work. That energy can never be faked; it comes from a commitment born of doing what you love and doing it for people who matter to you.

In life there are any number of responsibilities and obligations. We all have a quota of them—the stuff we need to do whether we want to or not. Passion is about moving beyond our obligations and on to those things we most love to do. They are usually the things we do best.

When you focus on things you really like to do, you are likely to do them with passion—and do them remarkably well!

Principles

What are the beliefs that allow you to shape your world (your performances) instead of being shaped by it?

Paul Johnson, the eminent British historian, wrote:

> *The best kind of democratic leader has just a few—*
> *perhaps three or four—central principles to which he is*

> *passionately attached and will not sacrifice under any*
> *circumstances. . . . I am not impressed by leaders who*
> *have definite views on everything. History teaches it is a*
> *mistake to have too many convictions, held with equal*
> *certitude and tenacity. They crowd each other out. A great*
> *leader* [read: a person who is acting remarkably] *is*
> *someone who can distinguish between the essential and*
> *the peripheral—between what must be done and what is*
> *merely desirable.*

We've all heard the saying, He who believes everything believes nothing. That statement has become a cliché because it is rooted in truth.

The people I have known over the years who impressed me as remarkable have been unswervingly committed to their core values, ethics, and personal and spiritual beliefs. They haven't just talked about their beliefs—they have lived them. When what you say is reflected in and amplified by how you live, you are almost certain to live a remarkable life.

Persistence

In today's attention-deficit culture, persistence gets short shrift when we talk about success. But Rome wasn't built in a day, and neither is remarkable performance.

My friend the author Michael LeBoeuf once told me, "It takes fifteen years to become an overnight success. The good news is that those fifteen years go very quickly."

The good news is that achieving remarkable performance in

what you do won't take fifteen years. What it *will* take is persistence. Think how different the world would be—how many more remarkable people and performances there would be—if persistence was embraced by more people; imagine what it would be like if fewer people in this world refused to give up when they encountered challenges or obstacles.

Ernest Hemingway was a remarkable writer whose mantra was: "Above all, endure." While I love his work, I disagree with his viewpoint. Remarkable performers and people don't simply endure—they exercise persistence. They refuse to give in to despair, and they work hard at doing what is right. "Persistence" is a strategic word that suggests purposeful action—like the forward motion of an unstoppable fullback who will not stop churning his legs until he gets the first down.

Legal-thriller author John Grisham has sold more than 200 million books worldwide in thirty languages. But his first novel was rejected by twenty-eight agents and publishers. When a publisher finally accepted it, only five thousand copies were printed, one thousand of which Grisham purchased himself. He hawked those volumes out of the trunk of his car to bookstore owners to spread word of his work. With his second novel, *The Firm*, he became a number-one best-selling author, and the rest is literary history.

If you have somewhere to go and something to say, don't endure. Persist until you get the hearing. When you do, your performance will undoubtedly get the encore it deserves. In the words of Robert Half, "Persistence is what makes the impossible possible, the possible likely, and the likely definite."

Personalization

England's equivalent to America's *American Idol* is called *The X Factor*—referring, of course, to that elusive, indefinable "star" quality that separates one performer from the rest. I like to think instead of the "U Factor"—those qualities that make you *unique* among the world's performers.

The U Factor is not something you have to acquire or search for. It's something you already possess, and something no one else has. It's as personal as your fingerprints, your voice print, and a scan of your retina. It's how you use purpose, passion, principles, and persistence to make your actions *you*. No one else in the world is like you.

When a woman from my church visited the Dalits, a downcast and outcast caste in India, she asked a young girl what she wanted to be when she grew up. "I can't be anything," the girl replied sadly. She (understandably) believed that her place in India's rigid social structure was her lot in life, never to be changed. The woman spent considerable time encouraging this young girl to believe that not only could she become somebody, she already *was* somebody.

When we try to be everybody, we inevitably fail. But when we focus on being true to ourselves, we can't help but succeed.

Country music star Michael Peterson told me about his first day as a college freshman. Having been awarded a football scholarship, he had high hopes for his college career—until he ran into a six-foot-three, 315-pound member of the varsity team. "If that guy's a lineman," he thought, "I'm done for."

Michael asked his roommate about the player he had seen. "Don't worry about him," his roommate said. "He's our kicker.

He's big, but he never made it as a lineman because *he can't move people*."

The Point

The point of every remarkable performance is to move people in a positive way—in the workplace, at home, on the stage, or in the community. If we aren't moving people to a better place in their lives, whether materially, emotionally, spiritually, or intellectually, then we're missing the point.

EPILOGUE

At the beginning of this book, I included the quote from Shakespeare's *As You Like It* that all the world's a stage and we are merely players upon it. Throughout the book, I have suggested that we can choose to make our performances remarkable. Whether we're "mere" players or serious players is completely up to us.

Each day men and women who are mere players take the stage unaware. They give little thought to their various roles and performances. This lack of awareness accounts, at least in part, for performances that are quite forgettable. We encounter people each day who appear to be sleepwalking through life.

The serious players know that what they do matters. Our performance is what we do each day in the many and varied roles of our lives. We take what we do seriously because we know we derive meaning from the things we do and how well we do them.

I hope you've learned some new ways to take *your* performance from mundane to memorable, from routine to remarkable.

By bringing passion, excellence, and joy to your performances, you are sure to invoke the Encore Effect—you will be called back time and again.

May all your performances be remarkable.